COMPLACENCY

CRITICAL
ANTIQUITIES
A SERIES EDITED BY BROOKE HOLMES AND MARK PAYNE

Complacency

CLASSICS AND ITS DISPLACEMENT
IN HIGHER EDUCATION

JOHN T. HAMILTON

The University of Chicago Press

CHICAGO AND LONDON

The University of Chicago Press, Chicago 60637

The University of Chicago Press, Ltd., London

© 2022 by The University of Chicago

Published 2022

Printed in the United States of America

31 30 29 28 27 26 25 24 23 22   1 2 3 4 5

ISBN-13: 978-0-226-81863-4 (cloth)

ISBN-13: 978-0-226-81862-7 (paper)

ISBN-13: 978-0-226-81864-1 (e-book)

DOI: https://doi.org/10.7208/chicago/9780226818641.001.0001

Library of Congress Cataloging-in-Publication Data

Names: Hamilton, John T., author.

Title: Complacency : classics and its displacement in higher education /
  John T. Hamilton.

Other titles: Classics and its displacement in higher education |
  Critical antiquities.

Description: Chicago ; London : The University of Chicago Press, 2022.
  | Series: Critical antiquities | Includes bibliographical references
  and index.

Identifiers: LCCN 2021061640 | ISBN 9780226818634 (cloth) |
    ISBN 9780226818627 (paperback) | ISBN 9780226818641 (ebook)

Subjects: LCSH: Classical philology. | Classicism. | Learning and
  scholarship.

Classification: LCC PA37 .H36 2022 | DDC 001.2—dc23/eng/20220210

LC record available at https://lccn.loc.gov/2021061640

♾ This paper meets the requirements of ANSI/NISO Z39.48-1992
(Permanence of Paper).

I am not held in esteem
I am not the stuff of dreams.

I am a place to put things.

People look at the figures
They trace on my face
But look right through me.

What would happen
If I threw myself open?

GUILLEVIC, "PLANE (I),"
TRANS. RICHARD SIEBURTH[1]

Contents

The Wolf on the Plain

Pleasing oneself may have unpleasant consequences. Since antiquity, moralists have stressed how contentment with present circumstances—with one's accomplishments and status—generally proves to be misleading and dangerous, in conflict with a reality that should serve as a sobering corrective. Just as flatterers employ pleasantries to mollify or persuade otherwise recalcitrant minds, so do self-satisfied individuals adhere to what they find pleasing in themselves to confirm their belief that every-thing is fine just the way it is. Just as seducers withhold critical information from their targets, so do self-deceivers gloss over any evidence that might contradict or compromise their high opinion of themselves, suppressing unwelcome news while exaggerating aspects that are reassuring and facilitating. Imperturbable self-confidence and vainglorious boasts may have a winning effect in society; victories that result from self-fabrications may for a while certify their profitability; yet ultimately, at least in a world perceived to be just, one would expect a final reckoning. For those who have grown too comfortable in their success, for those who actually believe in the overblown image they have contrived for themselves, retribution would constitute a crucial moral lesson, one that would put an end to all the deceptive games.

The moral lesson is clear, transmitted through numerous fables in the Aesopic tradition—a *classic* exemplum in every sense, and not simply because it is as relevant today as it was in the past.

Λύκος πλανώμενος <ποτ᾽ > ἐν ἐρήμοις τόποις,
κλινόντος ἤδη πρὸς <κατά>δυσιν ἡλίου,
δολιχὴν ἑαυτοῦ τὴν σκιὰν ἰδὼν ἔφη
λέοντ᾽ ἐγὼ δέδοικα, τηλικοῦτος ὤν ;
πλέθρου δ᾽ ἔχων τὸ μῆκος οὐ θηρῶν ἁπλῶς
πάντων δυνάστης ἀθρόων γενήσομαι ;
λύκον δὲ γαυρωθέντα καρτερὸς λέων
<ἑλὼν> κατῆσθι᾽ ὁ δ᾽ ἐβόησε μετανοῶν
οἴησις ἡμῖν πημάτων παραιτία.[1]

Once, when a wolf was wandering in deserted places,
as the sun was already beginning to set,
upon seeing his long shadow, he said:
"I am afraid of a lion, although I am so large?
Having a length of one hundred feet, shall I not plainly
Become lord of all the hordes of animals?"
But as the wolf boasted, a powerful lion
seized and devoured him: and the wolf cried, reflecting:
"Conceit is partly the cause of our sufferings."

In regarding his elongated shadow as a true representation of
his size, the wolf makes a lethal cognitive error: He takes himself to be greater than he in fact is; and this failure to distinguish reality from a merely visual effect causes him to overlook
the lion that is lurking on the plain. The wolf's inflated opinion
of himself has made him so cocksure that he no longer fathoms
the danger of the situation. Thus, even though he falls prey to a
voracious beast, the wolf is complicit in his own demise, having
traded in a once prudent fear for unsound recklessness. Because
the wolf's irresponsibility is partly responsible for his doom, the
sudden attack counts as condign punishment. With the excruci-
ating pain of the lion's fangs tearing deep into his flesh, the wolf
undergoes a radical change of mind: self-reproach replaces self-

deception. His own "conceit" (*oiēsis*), the wolf acknowledges, shares part of the blame. Yet this mental adjustment, this *metanoia*, does not occur soon enough for salvation. As in the case of the condemned man strapped to the grotesque machine in Franz Kafka's penal colony, the wolf's cognizance of his transgression coincides with his utter destruction.

The text has been attributed to Babrius, a poet presumably of Hellenistic Roman descent, living sometime between the first and second centuries CE in the eastern regions of the empire near present-day Syria. Metrical features indicate the author's grounding in Latin prosody, while allusions to Arabian customs exhibit a sound familiarity with Near Eastern culture.[2] As a fabulist, Babrius does not conceal the pedagogical intention of his work. In the prologue to the collection, he presents himself as an innovator who has rendered prose stories into Greek verse for a youth named Branchus, "having softened [*thēlunas*] the harsh lines of bitter iambics" (πικρῶν ἰάμβων σκληρὰ κῶλα θηλύνας, v. 18). The hint of femininity (*thēlus*) implicit in the verb for "softening" (*thēlunas*) underscores the author's aim to nurture innocent minds. The fables' content is to be transmitted in a tender, maternal tone, in stark contrast to the sarcasm and venom typically associated with the Ionian iambics of Archilochus and Hipponax. Consequently, according to ancient testimonies, already by the early third century, Babrius enjoyed a reputation as an effective instructional source for offering useful advice that emphasized internal thought processes and how these judgments might clash with life experience.

Fables have always been endorsed for tutorial purposes. Writing in 1883, William Gunion Rutherford, reader at Balliol College, Oxford, warmly recommended Babrius, whose "simplicity of style," together with "the careful regularity of his scazon," "have not only a literary value, but deserve a place in the history of educational methods."[3] The story of the wolf who proceeds with a false sense of grandeur and meets a brutal end plainly speaks to this didactic value.

In approaching an Aesopic fable, one expects the edifying moral that defines the genre, a useful illustration of how things ought to be. The lesson should be straightforward and universally applicable, a classic gem of time-tested wisdom, which rhymes well with ethical precepts handed down from antiquity: how "practical intelligence" (*phronēsis* or *dianoia*) should correct mere "opinion" (*doxa*) or "conceit" (*oiēsis*); how self-assessment should always be realistic and honest; how disillusionment often arrives too late, only as a painful "afterthought" (*metanoia*). Babrius thus presents the wolf as a negative exemplum, whose behavior should be avoided. Fascinated by his own gratifying shadow, the wolf epitomizes the kind of "self-absorption" or stubborn "self-will" (*authadeia*) that limits his ability to take notice of what lies before him. In recalling the famous allegory from Plato's *Republic*, the wolf, who takes a two-dimensional, projected silhouette for reality, is torn from the world of semblances, forced out of the darkness of deception and into the blazing light of three-dimensional truth. The path is painful and should be salutary, yet the wolf's senses remain too long in the dark. The lion's ambush thus constitutes a fitting nemesis that ought to address every act of extravagant "self-pride" (*hybris*) or blind "delusion" (*atē*). A young pupil of any epoch, regardless of cultural background, would indeed find much to take to heart.

A schoolmaster might permit a moderate sense of glee in seeing the wolf get his just deserts, in watching him suffer from the very pain he frequently inflicted on others. While the wolf's combative ferocity might be admired when illustrated, for example, by the Myrmidons in Homer's epic (*Il.* 16.156–63), in classical texts the creature is often portrayed in a deprecatory manner: as a cunning deceiver (Aesch., *Ag.* 1258–60); as a ravenous cheat (Aristophanes, *Lys.* 628–29); or as a ruthless thief (Aristophanes, *Clouds* 351–52). In Plato's *Laws*, the figure of the wolf is used to describe the criminal who lacks all moral principles (906d), while in the *Republic* he serves as a metaphor of the bloodthirsty tyrant (565d4–566a4).[4] Throughout the *Aesopica*, the wolf is depicted as equally fierce yet at the same time not particularly intelligent and often quite gullible. However much he may try to be clever, the wolf's persuasive arguments and calculated plans are generally frustrated. His insatiable hunger may make him sharp-sighted, always on the lookout for fresh meat, yet in the poem examined here, it is precisely an act of vision that turns the hunter into the hunted: "Seeing his long shadow," the wolf is emboldened, without noticing that, by locking his own image within his horizonal scope, he may have already singled himself out for certain demise.

Today, the fable can still serve as a cautionary tale, specifically on the common vice of *complacency*. The English term is particularly apt. Built from the Latin verb *placere* (to be pleasing or satisfying, acceptable or agreeable) and the intensifying prefix *com-*, *complacency* has come to denote being inappropriately pleased with oneself or with a situation to the point where any change, reconsideration, or improvement is dismissed as unnecessary. It applies to those who are unreasonably confident when there is no real cause, when the measure of one's self-worth is incongruous with the measure of one's true value, when aestheticized images, of oneself and of the world, risk colliding with the reality principle.

Complacency signifies a manner of self-satisfaction that is obviously exaggerated. It does not entail a feeling of gratification when gratification is fully warranted but rather ensues from placing too much trust in how one views things, ignoring outside advice and refusing to think differently. Complacent subjects refuse to change course when change is necessary. Although this pejorative sense of complacency is entirely modern, one can discern the moral failing in the wolf's blithe contentment with the way things appear, in his ill-founded pretensions, in his inability to examine and understand his limitations and vulnerability. Like the wolf, the complacent are bound to be mocked for convincing themselves of their superiority, for believing that their present self-image confirms their preeminence rather than being the result of contingency, arbitrary good fortune, or a mere effect of the sun's light.

Complacency thrives on inattentiveness. The afflicted are regarded as resting so pleasantly on their laurels that they miss out on golden opportunities, be it for profit or for redemption. Babrius's concluding depiction of the wolf's belated reconsideration (*metanoōn*) recalls how the tradition personified Metanoia as the dark companion to Kairos or Occasio. In one of his ekphrastic epigrams, Ausonius thus describes Pheidias's statue of the goddess Opportunity with frightful Metanoea at her back: as Occasio herself proclaims, "When I have flown away Metanoea remains; those whom I have passed by hold on to her" (*quandoque volavi, haec* [sc. Metanoea] *manet; hanc retinent, quos ego praeterii* [*Ep.* 33.13–14]). Nestled in the comfort of self-satisfaction, bedazzled by the light of self-aggrandizement, the complacent lose out, holding on to nothing more than regret.

The image of the extended shadow illustrates the discrepancy between reality and self-conception. The wolf mistakes a two-dimensional, distended projection to be evidence of his true size and mass. Overly content with this false self-appraisal, he struts across the open plain without recalling that the sun will set, without anticipating that his grand shadow will soon disappear into the night. Moreover, the flat, magnified shadow deludes him to regard the plain before him as an even, unthreatening course. *The flatness of the shadow correlates to the flatness of the plain.* In gazing at his enhanced appearance, the wolf thinks he can coast across the region free of any obstructions, impediments, or hazards that might confront or test his powers—"wandering [*planōmenos*] in isolated or empty places." The verb for "wandering," *planasthai*, concisely depicts the wolf's conviction that he is proceeding upon clear, level ground, one that allows for uninhibited "movement" or unrestricted "roaming" (*planē*). Perhaps Babrius, who often resorts to Latinisms, is exploiting the homophony between this Greek noun for wandering, *planē*, and the Latin adjective *planus*, which describes anything "flat," "even," or "smooth": *planasthai* as *per planum ire*, to walk across a level, easy passage, one that is free from danger.

In finding the region to be deserted or obstacle-free (*erēmos*), the wolf confirms for himself a feeling of power, which encourages him to ask, "Shall I not plainly [*haplōs*] become lord over all the hordes of animals?" The exclamation, however, betrays his delusion. The *wish* to "become" king underscores the fact that he is not king. Furthermore, what kind of power can be accorded to a sovereign of an explicitly unpopulated territory? The desire to be lord, therefore, should not be taken so "simply" or "plainly" (*haplōs*). Rather, it is the wolf's complacency that encourages his overreach. He comes to believe that he deserves the royal title, not by *changing* who he is or what he does, but rather by *remaining* exactly the same and staying the course. What might stand in the way of this self-investiture? Like a "wandering star" or *planet*, he floats at will through a heaven of his own making, feeling as divinely unencumbered as Mars or Jupiter. It is, indeed, pleasing (*placens*) to traverse an area without restriction, without worry. Yet of course, deep down, the wolf knows there are lions in these regions—*hic sunt leones*; he explicitly acknowledges a fear of these merciless predators ("I am afraid of a lion?"); yet the grand flatness of his shadow remains highly seductive. And so, the *lykos planōmenos* hovers over the landscape until the final catastrophe—the only true change in the fable—when the erstwhile star falls into the claws of the beast that has been spying on him all along.

"I [*egō*] am afraid of a lion?"—The evocation of a former but now conquered fear coincides with the wolf's explicit self-identification as a subject of language, as an emphasized *ego* that governs discourse and therefore putatively governs the plain. Egocentricity should legitimize the presumption of becoming "lord." Again, the wolf's flat body image blends deceptively into the evened region. The one planar phenomenon melds with the other, just as the one conclusion (self-aggrandizement) provides the basis for the next (a danger-free zone). Enticed by the shadow he casts before him, the wolf smooths out his sense of reality, just as his subjecthood integrates his sense of self. Any reminder of his limitations, anything that might contradict his distorted sense of power, is leveled out. This leveling of reality reinforces the unruffled portrayal that he takes as a genuine reflection of his stature. As the result of the late afternoon sun, the lengthened shadow may even suggest how a complacent trust in one's invulnerability often occurs at the zenith of a successful career, when expertise sees no reason for revision.

The flatness (*planitudo*) of the plain underwrites the wolf's complacency. Both the two-dimensional shadow and the landscape's surface admit no depth. Any internal doubt or worry, as well as any external bump or hindrance—anything that might disturb these smooth façades—has been paved over, however dubiously. This merger of self-evaluative and perceptive horizons, this pathetic fallacy, vividly evokes a central theme of the present study—namely, the relationship between notions of flatness and conceptions of complacency.

Thanks to idiosyncratic features of the English language, one can already hear the word *place* in the term *complacency*. *Place* is derived from Latin *platea*, which itself comes from the

Greek adjective *platus* (flat, even, smooth). Specifically, *platea* is a Latin borrowing from the Greek *hodos plateia*, "a broad and flat road," a thoroughfare with a hard-packed surface designed for smooth and convenient movement, free of any obstacle that might cause the pedestrian to falter. Over time, *platea* came to denote a leveled courtyard, and then a public square designed for congregation, open communication and exchange.

Across the centuries, however speculatively or fancifully, the *pla-* sequence that connects words of flatness (*platus*, *plax*, *planus*) with verbs of pleasing (*placere*) and soothing (*placare*) seems to exhibit a mimetic force, as if there were some inherent, natural relationship between pleasantness and evenness. This persistent paronomasia suggests a core metaphor—namely, that the feeling of being pleased relates to the experience of walking upon an open area with no threat of stumbling, that one is pleased in alighting upon a smooth, even surface where everything sits in an orderly place, where communication and transportation can proceed unimpeded. Well into the twentieth century, historical linguists have asserted this link between the flat and the pleasing, between *plax* and *placere*.[5] And although appeals to this *figura etymologica* have since found no basis in current linguistic science, its long-standing effects are operative throughout the tradition.[6]

The relationship makes intuitive sense. Complacency, one could say, flattens out experience and consequently leaves us flat. The Babrius fable is already suggestive in this regard. Perfectly content with his present self-image and discounting any evidence that would diminish his self-estimation, the wolf traffics solely in superficial appearances. Analogously, the complacent act as though the world does not exist in three-dimensional space—that there are no interior depths below the surface, that space is not voluminous and filled with perilous hideouts. They fail to acknowledge that there may be something more, something latent or secret, both in others and in themselves. Defined as a lack of depth, flatness eradicates all manners of negativity. The complacent *flatter* themselves into believing that they can proceed through life without engaging in the negative forces that reside behind or beneath what is positively present. They neglect what is spatially unseen as well as what is temporally absent. For both depth and time introduce an additional dimension, a conflicting plane of reality, which furnishes a reserve of negativity—the *not-here*, the *no-longer*, the *not-yet*—a powerful cache that would only upset smooth procedures and frustrate convenience, causing the kind of self-doubt, suspicion, and fearful hesitation that complacency glosses over.

In avoiding negativity, the complacent subject also averts radical otherness, the *not-me*. Again, the egotistical wolf fancies he could be "lord," yet only over a "desolate" realm. Isolation suits the wolf, who is typically portrayed as a loner. For him, all other living entities are prey and nothing more. He belongs to no community, insofar as a community is defined as a collective of subjects with different perspectives and different aims. *Self*-reflection is not only sufficient in making the wolf pleased with himself, it is also a guarantee that this pleasure will not be spoiled.

Complacency flourishes on sameness and withers on difference, and therefore it promotes conformity; for conformity, too, judges that otherness is without significance or value. When extended to society at large, complacency seems to endorse a constant repetition of the same—the norm toward which moral systems often aspire.

By ignoring the negativity of time, depth and alterity, complacency remains unaware of shifting circumstances. It reduces time to a standstill, space to what is visible on the surface, and otherness to a mere variant of sameness. Accordingly, the wolf fails to foresee the lion hiding around the corner; he fails to recall that the sun moves on a temporal course. He prefers to remain fully in the present, where everything is laid out *pleasantly*, entirely *ex-plained*, as if neither the past nor the future, neither what is below nor above the plain, could ever upset his prideful sense of self. Tellingly, the verb *planasthai* not only denotes free roaming in a general sense but also, like Latin *errare*, "to wander off," "to be led astray," "to be deceived."

*

A disparagement of complacency appears to accord with universally valid and therefore timeless, *classical* precepts. Regardless of cultural background or historical heritage, it would seem to be the case that one must always beware of becoming too pleased with oneself, that one must always guard against delusion, that one must always refrain from making inaccurate assessments of one's capacities. The legitimacy of these lessons is grounded in the conviction that they propound an objectifiable truth or law of nature as opposed to expressing a merely conventional, subjective, or contingent viewpoint. Classical criteria, therefore, have consistently provided an efficacious *platform* for imperial ambitions; for both the classic and the empire are presented as perpetuities impervious to mundane vicissitudes.

Claiming alliance with classical verities constitutes a powerful means for authenticating a nation's ideology. It can allow an entire population to defend itself against the accusation that its particular standpoint is but a presumption. As William Gunion Rutherford, quoted in the previous section, emphasized in 1883, Babrius is educationally effective. For late nineteenth-century pupils reading classics at Eton or Harrow, one could imagine how his fable promulgates hierarchies of innate power, like the one that subordinates the savagery of wolves to the nobler strength of lions. Would the formidable beast that arrives to chastise the wolf not recall the bravery of the British Empire, which advanced eastward beneath the banner of the Barbary Lion, just as Richard the Lionheart once marched against Saladin? Future administrators of the British colonies might have believed that an unequal distribution of power is perfectly natural and therefore legitimate, that studying the timeless classics is itself the earmark of a higher civilization, which would license dominance over purportedly less advanced cultures. The wolf's self-absorption could then be vilified as a perversion of courage, constancy or virtue; it could be disparaged as base selfishness, which undermines individual dignity, while deteriorating social and national cohesion; it could even characterize the parochial concerns of indigenous peoples as a serious threat to the imperial order.[7]

It is not difficult to discern the inherent contradiction that makes this position fragile and fallible. The allegation against the wolf's complacent credulity is suspiciously deployed to uphold one's own chauvinist perspective. Just as the wolf's delusions ignored the fact that his imperious shadow would vanish at dusk, so might pupils of the Victorian era never concede that, contrary to imperial propaganda, the sun might one day set on the British flag.

Although emphases may shift, any classical interpretation would arguably agree that Babrius's fable serves as an admonition that alerts readers to the deleterious effects of complacency. The moral message is transmitted *plainly*—without complication, without resistance, in Latin: *plane*. Yet precisely in this regard, the fable seems to set a trap. Like a wolf wandering across a deserted plain, readers travel across the flat page with the light of the classical tradition behind their back, filling the blank spaces of the text—the *erēmoi topoi*—with the projected shadow of their own imagination. The text thus becomes a smooth, easily traversed surface where one's preestablished knowledge can be pleasingly confirmed.

The fable, in other words, also functions as an allegory of reading. Before noticing it, the reader has gone from being an unobserved observer, nestled in the security of spectatorship, to becoming one of the dramatis personae on the story's stage. It may be pleasing to arrive at an unequivocal acceptation; it may be reassuring to acquire sound understanding; however, as Babrius's story demonstrates, the *pleasure* of presuming such knowledge puts the reader at risk. After all, it is the very comfort of proceeding untroubled and unchallenged that drives the wolf into horrific calamity. Readers who take the story as a negative exemplum may become too pleased with themselves, confident that they would never be as naïve or dim-witted as the fabular beast. They may be tempted to move through the text as if they were completely in the know and hence immune from ruin. Yet, thoroughly satisfied with their interpretations, they would be as imperiled as the wolf, about to succumb to the leonine power of other lines of thinking that may be crouching in the interpretive gaps.

Any moralist who is content to accuse others of complacency is open to the selfsame charge—not by being gratified with one's interpretation but rather by being *exceedingly* pleased with it, to the point where all other readings are dismissed out of hand. The conclusion that another is complacent is frequently proclaimed from a complacent position. Breaking out of this mental loop is difficult. In terms of the fable, in order to understand the moral and not be misled by one's own conceit, one has to read the narrative, which means, one has to read with the kind of conviction that brought the wolf to ruin. Paradoxically, to be unlike the wolf, one is compelled to follow in the wolf's tracks.

Whereas a *classical* reading would rest content with ascertaining a clear moral precept—an achievement that would supposedly make any subsequent interpretation superfluous—a *philological* approach would, in principle, remain dissatisfied with any and all conclusions. It would insist, explicitly or not, to keep every interpretation open. Philological concerns never cease to navigate through difficult textual histories, collating fragmentary evidence, questioning authorship, investigating possible literary sources and precedents, making judicious emendations and learned corrections, while striving toward the establishment of a readable text, albeit provisionally. The text as printed in the foregoing extract, extant only in a single fifteenth-century manuscript held in the Vatican Library, is after all the product of philological labor, much of which is speculative and open to further revision. Metrical inconsistencies or incongruities, usually the result of negligent copying over the centuries, require the addition of words, which the editor dutifully marks with diamond brackets (also known as angle brackets: < >), with variants consigned to the critical apparatus. These variants in themselves can be regarded as occupying the almost hidden lair of lions ready to pounce. Every word in the text is indeed open to debate, including the words that are inscribed in the codex. Yet, for a moral lesson to be clearly and usefully imparted, the philologist's critical urge must come to a halt. The desire to plumb the depths of any text must be curtailed so as not to disturb the even surface that bears the simple message. This resistance to critique, this insistence to adhere to the pleasing plane of straightforward sense, is precisely what is at stake in the problem of classical complacency.

If classicizing ambitions aspire toward timeless truth, philological pursuits adhere to time-bound, qualifiable truths. If a classical interpretation presumes to plane freely in some supernal realm, it can do so only on condition that all other readings remain mutely in place. In contrast, philology adheres to the bumpy, problematic field, tripping itself up, however unpleasantly.

That is not to say that philologists do not aim for definitive conclusions, nor have they been exempt from the charge of smugness. The road to classical complacency has often been paved with the best, most expert intentions. The point to stress, rather, is that philology runs the risk of becoming classically complacent whenever it forgoes its fundamental commitment to history, temporality, and difference, whenever it discounts contrary evidence that may subsequently come to light.

A philologically driven reading of the fable would turn to historical and cultural contexts, not only to resolve issues of dating or authenticity but also to engage in interpretations that would uncover the text's further ramifications. The philologist may investigate the semantic evolution of key terms; conventional definitions may be challenged or modified; Latinisms may be detected; the Greek versification may be examined for the influence of Latin prosody; archaeological evidence may be consulted. Structurally, such moves could be understood as analogous to the informational gestures of the classics schoolmaster who attempts to corroborate the fable's moral import by setting it within the broader classical tradition. Yet, whereas these classicizing acts of *placement* seek to promulgate determinations that are transhistorical and transcultural, philological investigations strive to keep the text fully within the dimension of time.

Philological insistence on historical context disturbs classicizing ambitions. If the nineteenth-century English classical curriculum proffered Roman governance as a virtuous model for Britain's vast colonial enterprises, Babrius's fable could potentially serve as a troubling critique. Living and teaching on the eastern outskirts of the empire, Babrius may or may not be alluding to the Romans' mythological kinship with the wolf, beginning with *Lupa Capitolina* who suckled the Eternal City's legendary founders. Perhaps the fabulist is evoking Ovid's figure of Lycaon, the Arcadian king who believed he could outwit

Jupiter and was consequently turned into a wolf (*Met.* 1.216–39); or perhaps the ancient Lykaia festival, which notoriously entailed human sacrifice. Are the Roman authorities not like the wandering wolf, the *lykos planōmenos*, who moves imperiously on the plain? Do they not exhibit a satisfied air as they march across vast regions presumed to be free of danger or resistance? If Rome's military prowess flattened out local differences and foreign customs to create a homogenized Syria Palaestina, would the resultant smugness not delude these colonizing legions into believing that they were greater and more powerful than they were, blinding them to threats that were nonetheless present, making them too self-absorbed to notice the tall lions that still adorned the ancient Arabian temples? Would they not one day regret their miscalculations, arriving too late to the realization that the world is not flat at all, or at least not as flat as they had imagined?

Sin in the Academy

In 2009, for a piece published in *Times Higher Education*, Matthew Reisz, an Oxford-trained classicist, invited several prominent professors in the United Kingdom to offer their views on "The Seven Deadly Sins of the Academy." Simon Blackburn, professor of philosophy at Cambridge University, selected "Complacency" for his contribution. That *complacency* would appear in a catalog of scholarly depravity should certainly come as no surprise. Like the fabular wolf, complacent scholars coast comfortably on past successes, incapable of recognizing anything wrong with present circumstances or any deficiencies in their behavior.

Elaborating on this general sense, Blackburn defines *academic* complacency as "the attitude that one's undoubted distinction in one's own subject entitles one to pontificate about any other; and conversely, that their ignorance of one's own subject disqualifies everyone else from having a worthwhile opinion on anything at all."[1] Thus construed, complacency exhibits an impertinence that damages scholarship in two distinct but related ways: first, by *overreach*—by believing that a single set of inquiries, methods, and criteria can arbitrate legitimately across the faculties; and second, by *contempt*—by dismissing all other approaches as useless or inconsequential. This dual aspect of complacency is academically sinful because it aims to exercise tyrannical, totalitarian control over the production of knowledge. Complacent scholars behave as though their disci-

pline constituted both an impenetrable fortress and an imposing watchtower: maintaining the way things are by keeping a
close eye on and refusing entry to all alien agents, by prohibit-
ing any *arrivant* from introducing differing dimensions to one's
area of expertise.

As Blackburn goes on to suggest, the offense is most prevalent today among mathematicians and natural scientists.

> Petted and rewarded from an early age for going through
> their particular hoops, daily seeing themselves unquestion-
> ably better at jumping through those hoops than all their
> peers, no more faulted for knowing nothing else than a
> champion golfer is faulted for his football skills, can they be
> blamed for assuming the mantle of omniscience?[2]

Current institutional, cultural, and social values are claimed to
be responsible for privileging one manner of scholarship above
the rest, for deciding what is and is not relevant. If the natural
sciences and mathematics receive the greatest emphasis in our
secondary school curricula, it is ostensibly because policymak-
ers have somehow been persuaded that competency in so-called
STEM fields (science, technology, engineering, and mathematics) matters more than proficiency in others. As a consequence,
skills in empirical observation, scientific method, and quanti-
tative reasoning are accorded top value. These are the "hoops"
that today demand the most rigorous training; and pupils who
master this instruction earn the highest praise—a process that
may eventually breed delusions of "omniscience," whereby academic success in allegedly superior subjects warrants the pre-
tension of success in inferior subjects. The resultant complacency fails to realize that expertise in one field does not perforce
translate into triumph in another, that a golfer who dominates
the fairway might strike a pathetic figure on the football pitch.

It is not difficult to appreciate Blackburn's concern. As a moral philosopher who presumes some degree of human freedom, he would be troubled to see a researcher reduce all ethical problems to merely physical causes, say, to matters of biochemistry or electrophysiology, just as he might hold out the hope that philosophical reflection might raise key questions and make vital contributions in the area of neuroscience. What Blackburn calls academic complacency points essentially to the problem of interdisciplinary communication, how overreach and contempt, which are based on delusions of self-sufficiency, foreclose opportunities for true intellectual exchange.

According to Blackburn, the present hegemony of mathematics and the natural sciences—their appeal to universal validity—is not itself universal. In nineteenth- and early twentieth-century England, this preeminence instead belonged to classicists who assured themselves, as well as most of the population, that "without years of Latin and Greek nobody could govern the colonies, but that with those years, anyone could."[3]

Most intellectual historians would corroborate Blackburn's claim that classics maintained a sovereign position in English academia throughout the Victorian and Edwardian eras. In the elite public schools that emerged in the wake of the Industrial Revolution, the classical-humanist tradition worked as a pipeline for transmitting stores of knowledge and power, and thus crystallized differences in social class: training in Latin was said to cultivate a meticulous and orderly mind, which thereby distinguished the middle from the working classes, while a profound engagement with ancient Greek transported the ruling class to realms of freedom well beyond mundane concerns.

In nineteenth-century England, the classical curriculum represented a normative standard for defining importance by setting up the necessary hoops and distributing ample rewards for those who learned to jump through them. It was classics alone which determined the benchmark for university education, grooming generations of scholars by way of exacting instruction to proceed through life complacently with a surplus of self-assurance. Such confidence lies in believing that what one knows corresponds perfectly to what is and has always been. In referring explicitly to the Victorian age, Christopher Stray underscores this ideal of perpetuity: "The invariant features of classics . . . relate to its construction from the symbolic resources of antiquity as an exemplary standard, something of permanent and general value able to resist the corrosions of change and relativity."[4]

One can also understand how the purportedly civilizing power of the classical curriculum could relate to the role this training played in Britain's imperial and colonial enterprises, which placed its agents in a superior position by keeping others in a subordinate place. Inspired by Greek and Roman classics, elites were encouraged to emulate the great men of antiquity, their virtue, their morals, and their resolve. London effortlessly served as the new Rome, intelligent and wealthy enough to rule foreign peoples across the entire globe—a metropolis long destined to civilize the not-yet-civilized, to establish a thriving and lasting Pax Britannica, an *imperium sine fine.* Hovering over the earthly sphere as lords over their property, the self-styled omniscient classicist-cum-imperialist moved freely and transcendentally, buffeted by a divinely supernal, timeless force. The complacent scholar may feel like a *planetary* god, capable of transiting from one disciplinary constellation to another, without hindrances, without worries, utterly secure. Powerful institutions, like powerful people, traverse these places at their pleasure, but only on the condition that everyone else are kept to their places, restricted to colonial positions that are deemed in need of expert governance.

Blackburn's remarks constitute a bold suggestion. Although

the empirical-quantifying approaches of natural sciences and mathematics today are altogether distinct from the humanist-linguistic approaches of the classical curriculum of the past, one is asked to regard these two spheres of study as exhibiting a common proneness to academic complacency, so defined. One is invited to consider that classics and the way it intervened in nineteenth-century English culture, society, and politics somehow provided the template for the hard sciences of the present age, that both realms share certain features, despite all the historical, cultural, and methodological differences.

How valid, then, is Blackburn's striking proposal? And is *complacency* the adequate term? Can it be used to unite disciplinary approaches that are otherwise poles apart? Moreover, how might this specifically academic version of complacency relate to complacency more generally understood? To what extent might this scholarly sin correspond to the moral fault as it appears beyond university culture? To begin addressing these questions, it would be worthwhile attending to the flatness that informs conceptions of pleasing, the *place* in *complacency*.

Colonial Planning

Derived from Latin *planum*—taken as the *flat* page upon which one plots out an agenda or a design for action—a *plan* serves as an efficient device for navigating whatever may be encountered. A plan preinscribes the future, reducing it to the easy legibility of a single plane. It smooths out recalcitrant difference, contains what is otherwise uncontainable, and thereby enables the subject to proceed with certainty and resolve.

The onetime appeal of a classical education rested in large measure on its capacity to prepare young men for a life of leadership, to provide them with a serviceable program for understanding and managing their world, to teach them how to relate whatever happens back to the already known. If this kind of classicism bred complacency, it is because it inculcated the belief that there is nothing new under the sun, that any fresh way of thinking is but a footnote to what has already been thought—all of which implies that there was nothing left to be done, save for maintaining what had already been set in place. For the complacent, fresh experiences are made to fit into the prepositioned plan or else are left to languish unnoticed.

By 1861, George Otto Trevelyan, the nephew of the statesman and historian Thomas Babington Macaulay, had breezed through his schooling at Harrow, earned second place in the classics honors course—the Tripos—at Trinity College, Cambridge, and published his first and only play, a cheeky drama in verse entitled *Horace at the University of Athens*. Within months after graduating, having achieved high marks in the competitive examination for the Indian Civil Service, he sailed to the subcontinent to work as secretary for his father, who was then serving as governor and finance minister in Calcutta (now Kolkata). Throughout this period, Trevelyan recounted his colonial experiences in a series of letters initially printed in *Macmillan's Magazine* and later collected in a single volume, *The Competition Wallah* (1864). Among the many vivid reflections, one episode in particular stands out. It was an early morning in April when he was rudely awakened by a "hideous din"—a cause for serious alarm, at least until his Indian servant, bearing the tea tray, informed him that it was no military battalion but rather the start of the "festival of Cali." As quickly as possible, Trevelyan gathered himself and headed to the street:

I seemed to have been transported in a moment over more than twenty centuries, to the Athens of Cratinus and Aristophanes. If it had not been for the colour of the faces around, I should have believed myself to be on the main road to Eleusis in the full tide of one of the Dionysian festivals. The spirit of the scene was the same, and at each step, some well-known feature reminded one irresistibly that the Bacchic orgies sprung from the mysterious fanaticism of the far East. . . . It was no chance resemblance this, between an Hindoo rite in the middle of the nineteenth century, and those wild revels that stream along many a Grecian bas-relief, and wind round many an ancient Italian vase; for every detail portrayed in these marvellous works of art was faithfully represented here.[1]

Trevelyan's training in classics has armed him with the power of metaphor that employs the familiar to express the unfamiliar. His extensive reading of ancient authors mediates his interaction with his new surroundings, furnishing him with an *explanatory* model that allows him to interpret what he observes in a meaningful fashion. As a consequence, this understanding confirms his position of sober mastery over the fanatic masses—an intellectual proficiency that would authorize Britain's imperial presence in India.[2] Within this sovereign perspective, historical time and distance collapse into a single graspable moment. Difference is flattened into the same.

Like the Roman wolf in Syria, the Cantabrigian scholar in India may be charged with the complacency of neglecting any evidence that might contradict his self-image or the legitimacy of colonial rule. Both submit to the convenience of a smoothened reality. Again, the wolf's amplified self-image, no less than Britain's global empire, depends on the delusion that the sun never sets. Yet, whereas the flattening ascribed to Babrius's wolf has to do with an epistemological failure, that which applies to Trevelyan points to a flat affect, the evened composure required for English civil servants. The *nothing-new* that characterizes the classical curriculum translates into the sangfroid of imperial administrators who are not to be surprised in foreign situations, no matter how bizarre or "hideous." Regarding Calcutta as ancient Athens fortifies the security of the colonial agent, who is thereby protected against the menacing aura of difference. It allows Trevelyan to dismiss "the colour of the faces" so that he can rest assured in a climate of whitewashed sameness.

Although a nineteenth-century classical education might have promoted such haughty dismissals, the very nature of this plan speaks against basic pedagogical ideals, at least those that would encourage a more honest, less complacent grappling with difference.

In 1884, while serving as headmaster at the City of London School, Edwin A. Abbott addressed the problem of intellectual complacency in Victorian society in his satire *Flatland: A*

Romance of Many Dimensions. The work, published pseudony-
mously, presents a purely two-dimensional world, narrated by
a figure named A. Square, who painstakingly describes how a
reality without depth might appear and function. Class distinctions are fixed and clearly identifiable by variations of angular-
ity in each of the plane figures. Men in the lowest classes, the
soldiers and workers, are isosceles triangles, while those in the
middle class are equilaterals; professionals are squares, and
their children are pentagons; the nobility starts with hexagons
and ascends to more complex polygons. Women, however, are
simply lines, without angles and therefore without rationality.

Of course, since they exist on a plane, every person appears
as a line. Still, educated minds are able to determine angle variations by observing the speed at which the edges of the line fade
off into the foggy atmosphere. Oblivious to the fact that they are
confined to a single plane, the Flatlanders get on perfectly well.
A. Square pities the shortsightedness of the king of Lineland,
who stubbornly refuses to believe in a second dimension. In
vain, the narrator tries to instill common sense in the monarch.

These reflections form the basis for A. Square's own initial confusion when he is suddenly transported to Spaceland
and encounters solid shapes for the first time: "I looked, and,
behold, a new world!"[3] Yet, as the narrator ultimately discovers, the world is not *new* at all but rather the very *same* world,
only now with an additional dimension, never before perceived.
Depth perception results from stereoscopy. Upon returning to
Flatland, the enlightened narrator cannot persuade his fellow
citizens of a third dimension and is forthwith imprisoned for
life. He writes his memoires, so to speak, de profundis.

Abbott's mathematical fantasy aimed to introduce the concept of the fourth dimension to his late nineteenth-century
readership. Rigorously trained in classics at St. John's College,
Cambridge, Abbott taught comparative philology, while indulg-

ing his taste for non-Euclidean geometry, in particular the work of Charles Howard Hinton, who published his article "What Is the Fourth Dimension?" in 1880.[4] For Abbott, the moral implications were clear: There is great value in disturbing one's disciplinary basis by welcoming other modes and paradigms of thinking. New knowledge arrives whenever one sees things in a way other than before, whenever one *plane* of perception is intersected by another. Thus, in entertaining recent mathematical theories, the classical philologist stirred himself out of complacency. He would no longer be one of those "Slaves of our respective Dimensional prejudices."[5]

Had Abbott's compatriot, George Otto Trevelyan, the ethical temperament to realize his own dimensional prejudices, he might have undergone a true conversion or metanoia, coming to see the inhabitants of India as people in their own right rather than mere illustrations of a preinscribed plan, fixed well beforehand at a considerable distance.

Propositional Surfaces

Nothing is more fragile than a surface.

GILLES DELEUZE, *LOGIC OF SENSE*

Insofar as ethics concerns how human subjects *act* in the world, complacency, regarded specifically as a disposition that acts while refusing to act differently, is an ethical fault. Ethics is concerned with how one ought to behave, not only in order to accomplish deeds that correlate to one's principles, but also to change when a conflict arises. For this reason, ethics is unthinkable without a full consideration of personal values, which motivate the choices and actions that aim to improve the situations in which we find ourselves. Lacking the capacity to evaluate alternative options, the human subject falls into indecisiveness. Thus, William Shakespeare's Hamlet cannot act in his confrontation with Claudius, explicitly because his life has lost all value: "How weary, stale, flat and unprofitable / Seem to me all the uses of this world!" (*Hamlet* 1.2.133–34).[1] Values are required to make decisions, to approve one course of action over another, to distinguish the better from the worse. The stale flatness of Hamlet's perspective condemns him to melancholic torpor, to a strange complacency so severe that he is incapable of doing anything about it.

The absence of values, however, is not the only case that inhibits active improvement. In Simon Blackburn's broader philosophical project, the risk of complacency attends any moral-realist position that confuses David Hume's key distinction between *fact* and *value*. Ethics has long been based on the understanding that moral judgments are not cognitive beliefs about how the world is but rather conative reactions that express how the world ought to be. The problem is how to reconcile perceptible facts and normative values.

Moral realists resolve this problem by asserting that ethical statements are propositional, that they directly refer to objective properties independent of subjective viewpoints. Predicates like "right" and "wrong" can be determined and ethical behavior can be justified, provided one's behavior conforms to moral facts that are secure and certain. In his work on metaethics, Blackburn consistently interrogates this very principle of moral realism by pressing the Humean division between fact and value. All the same, Blackburn's approach also argues against all varieties of *antirealism*: against eliminative materialism, which regards moral notions as neurological effects; against error theory or nihilism, which rejects moralizing predicates as mere products of acculturation; against conceptual reductionism, which explains moral properties by turning to other, nonmoral discursive practices; against constructivism, which defines moral judgments as mind-dependent, as subjective representations that create the reality described; and also against neutralists who dismiss the entire debate as meaningless. In sum, Blackburn contests both realist and antirealist positions. On the one hand, he cannot condone the idea that moral knowledge is objectively ascertainable, while on the other hand he is unwilling to accept that moral knowledge is altogether impossible. He therefore tempers the extremes of realism and antirealism by developing what he calls *quasi-realism*.

Quasi-realism respects the viability of a moral truth without, however, sacrificing the *provisional* nature of each judgment. It is indeed possible—and cardinally important—to acknowledge the existence of right and wrong, yet these predicates cannot be allowed to settle into dogmatic inflexibility; they cannot be consigned to an immovable *place*. By ignoring the provisional nature of one's judgments, one straitjackets the very basis for practical change—that is, one becomes complacent.

Yet how can a provisional truth still be true? To address this matter, Blackburn reiterates the basic premise of his noncognitivism, that moral values must be strictly distinguished from objective facts. To clarify, Blackburn separates *inputs* and *outputs*. Inputs are *descriptive* representations of what the subject perceives to be factually true or false, while outputs are *directive* representations that the agent chooses to do on the basis of evaluative reasoning.[2] The natural world given to the senses, the world that can be observed and measured by the natural sciences, differs essentially from the normative realm of ethical practice.

This dualist analysis conflicts with the aims of more holistic thinkers such as John McDowell, who appears to revert to a realist stance by merging descriptive and directive aspects into a single, nonanalyzable "sensibility."[3] McDowell wants to offer a "thick" account of moral judgment—one that explicitly alludes to "all the whirl of organism Wittgenstein calls 'forms of life.'"[4] McDowell's sensibility theory thereby intends to explain how sensible, nonmoral description elicits an appropriate moral response; and it is precisely this intention that Blackburn criticizes.

The critique again depends on the fact/value distinction. To illustrate the shortcomings of McDowell's approach—the danger of unifying fact and value—Blackburn gives the example of "cuteness." One can imagine a man and his friends agreeing on features that constitute a woman's cuteness: perceptible features that elicit and also justify their affective responses. According to McDowell's account, those who disagree, including ethicists, can simply be dismissed: they simply do not see things the same way. Their sensibility may be wrongheaded, but it would still take some effort to persuade them to "just see" things differently. For Blackburn, however, by failing to distinguish the descriptive aspect from the directive, attitude-forming one, agents think and behave in a way that they feel is sheltered from moral criticism—a feeling that Blackburn finds highly questionable: "Now it is *morally* vital that we proceed by splitting the input from the output in such a case. By refusing to split we fail to open an essential specifically *normative* dimension of criticism."[5] If the criteria of female cuteness were to include a pleasant disposition or a readiness to be subservient, one would essentially characterize women in an atrocious manner, likening them to small children or house pets. Only when we break the judgment down into the component parts of description and expression can we focus on the men's dubious reaction and aim to correct it. As Blackburn remarks, "Once we can separate input from output enough to see that this is going on, the talk of whirls of organism, or single 'thick' rules, or a special perception available only to those who have been acculturated, simply sounds hollow: disguises for a conservative and ultimately self-serving complacency."[6]

For Blackburn, it is ethically insufficient to remark on what makes virtuous agents good and vicious agents bad. It is not enough to acknowledge that the righteous see things correctly, while the unrighteous do not. Rather, one must demonstrate that virtuous behavior means *reacting* virtuously. Moral realism deludes itself into presuming genuine knowledge about the world. It puts all trust in training, in learning how to recognize truth from falsehood. And on the basis of this training, it sees itself as impervious to critique. In Blackburn's view, this presumption is not only a failure to think but also a failure to change, a failure to improve, which functions as a shield of closed-minded complacency. It is analogous to the complacency of scientists whose training encourages them to arbitrate on every question without entertaining a critical contribution from someone who may see things another way. It is analogous to the complacency of nineteenth-century classicists, equally well trained, who believe they are authorized to govern the empire, untroubled by dissent voiced from other dimensions. In the end, these academically complacent scholars are as in thrall to flatness as Hamlet, not because they are without values but rather because they level the vital distinction between value and fact. Their sin is to rest on smooth, two-dimensional ground, secure in their beliefs and thus incapable of acting differently.

While this retreat into dogmatism must be rejected, there has to be a way to arrive at some kind of basis for evaluative reasoning. In Blackburn's view, subjective relativism or skepticism is just as damaging to the ethical enterprise as realist self-assurances:

> We have to know why to educate our child to be courageous, say, and this involves turning over the features involved, and, in the light of other attitudes of course, buttressing or undermining our commitment to it as a value. But this is not to say that either input or output is fixed by any kind of definition or purely linguistic convention. They are malleable, and change with the importance we attach to things and to our reactions to things.[7]

Accordingly, Blackburn has recommended considering the "propositional surface" of ethical thinking.[8] Inputs are still inputs and outputs are still outputs; conative-directive attitudes cannot be regarded as cognitive-descriptive beliefs; yet they nonetheless can be explained in a manner similar to the way we describe facts. Quasi-realism names precisely this "realistic-seeming" treatment of our moral reflections. It enables us to speak of moral knowledge, moral propositions, and moral truth, albeit in a provisional fashion.

The *propositional surface* is just as flat as the smooth ground on which complacently comfortable agents proceed through life, yet it is more like a discrete covering that is imposed on the judgment—something placed on top and therefore something *replaceable*.

If some of today's natural scientists, like yesteryear's classicists, succumb to academic complacency by presuming to stand on firm, flattened ground, quasi-realists maintain an implacable disposition by limiting their engagement with flatness to a propositional surface that works more like a long *plank* over a deep ravine: adequate as an interim device for grappling with moral knowledge yet without concealing the fact that every solution is but an ephemeral one, always subject to change. The propositional surface reminds us that knowledge, like a plank, is both firm and movable, presumably trustworthy but not permanent—simply a means to proceed. Should such knowledge ever harden into coherent, airtight doctrine, it would foreclose the need to think. Action would no longer be moral but rather conformist or even compulsory. Instead of being ethical agents, we would become thoughtless followers of some immutable plan. Conversely, should all moral knowledge turn out to be utterly delusional—altogether unreal—we could test our luck with a healthy leap, but always at the risk of plummeting into the abyss of nihilism.

Classical Platforms

On the surface self-assured and Parnassian in its dictates,
at a closer remove classicism reveals a number of interior fault lines.

JAMES I. PORTER, "FEELING CLASSICAL"

The past must be handled with care, lest one fall into a state of complacency. Excessive contentment with customs, conventions, and accepted norms bespeaks a conservatism that installs an idealized past to serve as an irrefutable standard against which new initiatives are mercilessly judged or outright discouraged. If the complacent appear comfortably priggish, it is because they see their lives as perfectly congruent with the way things are presumed to have always been. In their view, any substantial revision or bold reform is deemed unnecessary, if not entirely detrimental. This self-assurance may appear strong-willed, yet it conceals a profound fear of time, which may spell a reversal in fortune; for open-ended time is the dimension in which unwanted events can occur—events that could qualify, compromise, or destroy what has heretofore been attained. Hence, past practices are maintained as invariant models of perennial value. A critique of complacency would entail showing that, although established norms provide sure paths through life's endeavors and experiences, when adopted unreflectively, they become confining and restrictive, reducing further enterprises to a stagnant rehearsal of the same.

It is not surprising that Simon Blackburn identified nineteenth-century English classicists, together with today's math-ematicians and natural scientists, as exhibiting a propensity toward academic complacency. Although their methods and criteria differ vastly, their shared confidence is the product of rigorous training that could, but not inevitably, encourage the belief that their particular styles of thinking are neither particular nor stylistic at all, but rather consistently verifiable, correct, and universally applicable. Both might well be tempted to appeal to nomothetic principles that posit transcendent laws and absolute, unassailable truths immune from contingencies. Complacency obtains whenever experts, inflated by their prior success, operate under a realist assumption that their subjective values correspond directly to objective facts.

That is not to say that every Victorian classicist or every current scientist or mathematician is necessarily complacent, only that the tendency to be guided by fixed principles may be somewhat more likely in these cases. Moreover, it would be a mistake to claim that scholars who are judged complacent fail to produce knowledge. On the contrary, the zealous exertion of these teachers and researchers puts them at a far remove from the blind negligence and deficient action that are generally ascribed to this fault.

With academic complacency, new contributions are still acceptable, yet only when they exhibit a high degree of accommodation within a preordained framework. Complacency proffers a methodological *place* on which knowledge should be acquired, verified, and preserved—a normative flatland that is conceived to be perfectly sufficient, not in need of any innovations or supplements, particularly from other disciplines. The complacent scholar proceeds on a single plane, to which sole explanatory power is granted. Anything that may arrive from another, wholly novel dimension is dismissed as inconsequential.

If complacency is understood as a reverence toward past practices and established ideals, then an unreflective classicism does, indeed, pose a serious threat. Stubborn traditionalism ignores the demands of the present age and forecloses any substantive future, breeding conformism and sterile conventionalism. Such classicism overlooks the historically constructed nature of its values. It fails to acknowledge that its criteria are but the result of decontextualization, abstraction, and tendentious selection, which altogether smooth over the heterogeneity and contradictions found in the ancient legacy itself.[1] For this reason, classics as a discipline, no less than the natural sciences and mathematics, has long recognized the need to extricate itself from any form of classicism, from any pedantic position that rests exclusively on prior achievements and thereby doubts the validity of all departures from entrenched norms.

It is ostensibly the force of other disciplinary dimensions that underlie the paradigm shifts that redeem modes of knowledge from idling in the rut of complacency—from routine thinking that is often identified as *classical*. The so-called hard sciences have developed far beyond classical models of a mechanistic-deterministic nature by considering the nuanced variables of broader, more complex views. Classical mathematics similarly has been challenged by constructivism, intuitionism, and predicativism. In an analogous way, toward the latter half of the nineteenth century, the discipline of classics countered its classicizing tendencies by adopting scientific, philological methods presumed to be value-free and pluralistic.

*

Among German writers in the first half of the eighteenth century, dogmatic classicism came to be seen as enfeebling in its stiff guidelines, constraints, and criteria. A prime target was Johann Christoph Gottsched, who aimed to impose a poetics of strict, incontrovertible rules—an ironclad *Regelpoetik*, modeled explicitly on French neoclassical precepts. That Gottsched's Lutheran neighbors would memorialize him as the "pope of literature" (*Literaturpapst*) speaks volumes about his reception. Self-satisfied artists and writers like Gottsched were regarded as insufferably pompous, as deriving far too much pleasure from their own status. Utterly convinced that they already knew everything that must be known, these high priests of culture and taste seemed to presume the privilege of dictating their regulations on others, with little to no patience for any disputes or deviations.

Still, classicism remained highly alluring by being altogether pleasing. As Pierre Corneille proclaimed, "The goal of the poet is to please [*plaire*] according to the rules of his art."[2] Symmetry and balanced proportion, clarity and integral order, provide a sound basis for enjoyment and appreciation. It feels good to have one's expectations beautifully met, to recognize the logic that organizes a work of art, to find one's values and tastes brilliantly confirmed. Yet, although superb artists like Corneille understand how to produce pleasure by way of unpleasurable moments of tension and anxious incomprehension, lesser minds often withdraw into the cozy convenience of empty formalism. Epigones and unreflective imitators surrender to ready-made prescriptions without considering any need to tailor or replace. They desperately try to tuck their work into the Procrustean bed of their narrow, obstinate views. They lull their acolytes as they have lulled themselves into the complacency of being pleased at all costs, peddling contentment by avoiding confrontation and keeping things even keeled, which almost invariably means ignoring anything that might impinge on this comfort zone. Whoever disagrees—whoever is not pleased with being so pleased—is dismissed as an inexorable upstart.

Always ready for a good quarrel, modernism struggles to liberate itself from this debilitating trap. From the modernist perspective, what should be absolute, timeless, and universal cannot be an anemic corpus of abstract principles and decorous forms but rather human reason itself—the innate capacity to transcend the given and seek out the new, to identify problems and invent fresh solutions. Doctrinaire classicists, too, may appeal to reason in determining the ideals and standards that they promote as irrefutable. Yet for the modernist, such determinations quickly tend to congeal into a set of restrictions that hold progress back.

On the whole, modernizers do not discount the past at all, but rather regard it as a springboard for leaping into the future. Genial classical artists, like inspiring scholars of history, are implacably modern when they use the achievements of antiquity for criticizing current institutions and customs. Modernist aspirations consistently turned to antiquity for motivation to change the world. The rebellious nature of the multiple *querelles des anciens et des modernes* finds its precedent, after all, in a thoroughly classical source, in Tacitus's *Dialogus de oratoribus*. As Karl Marx underscored, the revolutions of the late eighteenth century would have been unimaginable without the formidable impulses of ancient republicanism. It was the Hellenism of Oscar Wilde and Virginia Woolf, of H.D. and Sigmund Freud, that audaciously deployed classical texts to challenge the status quo and incite an expansion of sexual mores, just as it was a profound and innovative engagement with Homer that spawned the radical reinvention of literature attributed to James Joyce's *Ulysses*.

Thus, the classics can always be evoked to overturn conventional thinking and shatter fixed worldviews.[3] Yet, to speak obliquely with Friedrich Nietzsche, there is a damaging abuse of history whenever a repertoire of past models is monumentalized to the point where they are no longer tested vis-à-vis the present with an eye toward next steps. The modernist is not averse to being pleased per se, as long as what pleases—*quod placet*—is deserving of approval. Otherwise, an adherence to prior accomplishments deteriorates into a fatal carelessness, into a stagnating security that is inattentive to changing circumstances and fresh demands.

The great era of French neoclassicism in the latter half of the seventeenth century—the artistic success of Corneille, Molière, and Jean Racine—testifies to a generally noncomplacent interaction: the qualification of the present by the past and the modification of the past by the present. Noncomplacent classicism is *bifocal*. It avoids the pitfalls of sterile formalism by negotiating two distinct historical-cultural planes. In this way, classicism promises to correct not only the dead end of monumentalism, which views antiquity as a restrictive blueprint, but also the impasse of antihumanism, which dismisses the past as wholly unimportant, long interred, and altogether forgettable.[4]

Reciprocal, bifocal action underwrites the very idea of *culture*. Derived from the perfect passive participle of *colere* (to care for, to dwell, to wait, to *cultivate*), *cultura* retains its initial agricultural sense of tilling the land, removing large stones, and preparing an even ground for sowing and harvesting. Embedded in the metaphorical substrate of the Latin lexicon is an anthropological conception of culture that harks back to the Neolithic transition from nomadic to sedentary life—to a life of fixed settlements that exhibit relative stability and continuity.[5] *Cultura* points to an engagement whereby human labor transforms wild nature into an evened site for something to grow and flourish, cultivated according to derived rules, seasonal rhythms and climatic variables, while requiring attentiveness to shifting conditions.

One can detect these acts of installation in the verb *plantare*, which is cognate with *planus*, denoting "to fix in place," to *plant* seeds by pressing them down with the "flat sole of the foot" (*planta*) and waiting patiently for the vegetation to sprout.

In this figurative sense, the nourishment that culture affords subsists in the plant life that grows from the carefully prepared soil. Although well-planned, in order to produce healthy sustenance, agriculture must engage in incessant toil. It cannot rest content with the fallow field, nor can it simply follow absolutely fixed routines. Culture requires a vertical intersection of the horizon. The plow digs deeply into the earth's surface, and the plant that supports life shoots up from the ground into the dimension of height. Fruitfulness results from the combination of two axes.

Correlatively, vital classicism involves a cultural orientation that mediates two differing dimensions, not spatially but rather temporally. The array of prior achievements recorded in literary and artistic history serves as a stable platform for productive work in the present. The classical artist "inhabits" or is "at home in" (*incolit*) two places divided by time, with each site acting on the other. As in the cultivated relationship to the gods in antiquity—the *cultus deorum*—classicism calls for repeated consultation with instituted authorities. As is often remarked, the earliest extant use of the adjective *classicus* is found in the *Noctes Atticae* of Aulus Gellius, who reports that, in questions relating to grammar, it is always better to confer with "any orator or poet, provided he be from an earlier cohort"—that is to say, one should consult a "writer of the highest class" (*classicus . . . scriptor*) rather than one of "the lowest" (*proletarius*; *Noct. Att.* 19.8). Status and precedence offer a guiding light whenever a particular problem is encountered in the present day; and it is this illuminating offering that composes the tradition.

Tradita—that which has been handed down or transmitted —recalls the nature of the "gifts" (*data*) that arrive "across" (*trans-*) the temporal distance. Along similar lines, notions of reception, which equally portray tradition as a gift, elicit gratitude as well as the desire to give in return, as if it were following the terms of the old cultic contract, *do ut des*, "I give so that you may give"—a binding agreement that should safeguard continued offerings from both parties. The classical tradition has always sown the conditions both for the survival of the ancient record and for fresh artistic initiatives. Within this framework of dispensation and compensation, present diligence grants perdurance to the ancient sources that in turn offer the current age some mode of transcendence.

A robust classicism is therefore capable of lifting participants from the confusion of the present era, but only from the standpoint of the present. The works of ancient authors and artists are mined for universal precepts that promise to assist modern artisans and writers to organize their approaches and thereby create coherent and efficacious works. It is vitally important, however, that every poet and painter, every sculptor or architect, choose the best rules, forms, and technical solutions for imitation. The modern artist is faced with a vast array of inherited options that must be assessed according to criteria of correctness and applicability. Through prolonged study and the rigorous training of sensibility, classical artists aim to glean what is pertinent or relevant to modern endeavors and disregard the rest. Mindful of the foregoing citation from Aulus Gellius, antiquity alone does not determine the "classical"; it must also demonstrate the highest qualities, distinguished from the throng of inferior, less useful traits. Classicism must be selective. The extensive store of materials left behind by artistic predecessors should not be regarded as worthy on the basis of antiquity alone. The classical artist should not embrace all that has been handed down, only that which proves fruitful for present enterprises—what Matthew Arnold famously characterized as "the best that has been thought and said."[6]

The renaissances that punctuate the West's literary and artistic histories have consistently provided the means for emancipating human expression from the restraints of religious dogmatism and social conventions. The appeal to perennial values reveals the path out of an otherwise directionless, anarchic modernity. In consulting the ancient authorities whose work surpasses the limitations of their own time, modern artists hope to discover a sure plan for overcoming their own time-bound restrictions. Although Latin and ancient Greek are historical languages, the aesthetic, moral, and philosophical lessons they impart are presented as ahistorical or suprahistorical, as eternally essential to humanity, as connecting the present plane with deathless verities. Cultivated principles and virtues—clarity and order, symmetry and balanced proportion, unity, decorum, and beauty—all refer to a realm that transcends the sublunar regions of ephemerality and difference, and thereby claim to provide models that can help us ascend these secure heights.

Yet, should ambitious poets decide on shortcuts, should they adopt any or all forms without applying sound judgment and honest toil, the road to artistic success is gravely threatened. As Nicolas Boileau-Despréaux formulates it at the head of his *Art poétique* (1674):

C'est en vain qu'au Parnasse un téméraire auteur
Pense de l'art des vers atteindre la hauteur :
S'il ne sent point du ciel l'influence secrète,
Si son astre en naissant ne l'a formé poëte,
Dans son génie étroit il est toujours captif :
Pour lui Phébus est sourd, et Pégase est rétif.
(ART POÉT. 1.1–6)[7]

It is in vain that, ascending to Parnassus, a daring author
Thinks the art of verse attains these heights:
If he does not at all sense from the heavens the secret influence,

If at birth his star has not made him a poet,
In his narrow genius he is always captive:
For him Phoebus is deaf, and Pegasus is restive.

In Boileau's depiction, the rash author is bound by time insofar
as he feels there is no time to spare. He is not willing to pause
and reflect on his art. He avoids testing the value of traditional
forms and instead chooses the quick and easy path by taking
these values at their word. One may presume that he is not a poet
at all insofar as he lacks the innate sensibility to distinguish
what is truly worthwhile from what is not. For Boileau, this key
recognition can only be the result of assiduous labor, which
carefully considers the precepts contained in the work of one's
predecessors and then attempts to accommodate them to present efforts. The impatient writer falls short of this ideal by opt-
ing for a clear plan that requires no poetic struggle. He travels
along a paved road, a hardened surface, convenient and stable,
yet one that prevents any true nourishment to sprout. That is
to say, he foolishly places all trust in a flattened understanding
of past achievements, one that does not call for intensive grappling, one that does not pose any serious problems, but rather
one that would allow smooth, unhindered movement toward a
goal that Boileau identifies as "vain."

Classicism degenerates into complacency whenever it provides itself with a past that has been plastered over for the sake
of untroubled convenience. Boileau understood that he himself
was not exempt from this kind of artistic failing. In the *Ninth
Satire* (1668), he admonishes his own "mind" or "wit" (*esprit*)
for resting on an established sense of criteria that no longer
receive the critical attention they demand:

C'est à vous, mon Esprit, à qui je veux parler.
Vous avez des défauts que je ne puis celer :

Assez et trop longtemps ma lâche complaisance
De vos jeux criminels a nourri l'insolence

(*SAT.* 9.1–4)[8]

It is you, my wit, to whom I wish to speak.
You have some faults that I am unable to conceal:
My weak complaisance has sufficiently and for too long
Nourished the insolence of your criminal games.

If classicism were to settle into "weak complaisance," reducing itself to a mere repertoire of hard-and-fast rules—renouncing the *discrimination* that draws a *critical* line (κρῖμα, *crimen*)—then it would commit the most "criminal" of artistic undertakings: surrendering to the tyranny of arbitrary formalistic rules that mire the writer in the very dogmatism that art promised to eliminate.

The temptation, of course, is great. The godlike nature of the ancient authorities threatens every cultic *do ut des* with an imposing asymmetry, capable of subordinating all present endeavors to past precedents. One might be led to imitate models apishly, when those models are taken to be unsurpassable. The rules can all too readily assume an indisputable quality, to the point where any mutual interaction would be deemed unwarranted. Once one becomes comfortably assured that the given method is perfectly correct, one proceeds without the bothersome questioning that characterizes real achievement. Boileau chastises his own cognitive faculty, his *esprit*, for having chosen the easier path. His complacency is "weak" or "cowardly" (*lâche*) because it often lets things pass (*lâcher*) without appropriate scrutiny, indulging in the sheer pleasure of assurance.

As already noted, the arousal of pleasure is a primary aim of the classicism that defined Boileau's era. Corneille's pronouncement, which posits the demand to please (*plaire*) as the highest rule, is corroborated by Molière and Racine and finally endorsed by Boileau: "The secret is first of all to please [*plaire*] and to affect [*toucher*]" (*Art poét.* 3.25). Here, the intention follows Horace, who famously recommends that poetry "be either useful or delightful" (*aut prodesse . . . aut delectare*; *Ars poet.* 333), or preferably a mixture of both (*miscuit utile dulci*; 343). Moreover, it recalls how Horace gratefully describes the effects of the inspiration received from the Muse Melpomene: *quod spiro et placeo, si placeo, tuum est*—"That I am inspired and pleasing, if I am pleasing, is because of you" (*Carm.* 4.3.24). Classical art pleases by presenting things in clear and symmetrically balanced order, by respecting decorum, by meeting genre expectations—by placing everything into a coherent, comprehensible and eminently satisfying array. Yet cowardly complacency obtains, whenever one comes to conceive the tradition as a foreclosed totality of immutable laws, whenever one puts all trust in past judgments without confronting them with present circumstances, whenever one rests content with the single plane of antiquity while ignoring the current dimension. Complacent theorists and artists are those who are so tranquilized by the pleasure of poetic assurances and conveniences that they deny the possibility of improvement. In these cases, the art of pleasing, the *ars placendi*, becomes a mere code of civility—a refined and polished surface that is smooth to the touch yet fails to be touching.

Like the staunchest moral realists, classicism's nonreflective adherents proceed as if it were possible to acquire objective knowledge of artistic virtues that are timeless and true. In his *Ninth Satire*, Boileau catches himself falling prey to this common epistemological mistake:

On croiroit, à vous voir dans vos libres caprices
Discourir en Caton des vertus et des vices,

Décider du mérite et du prix des auteurs.

(SAT. 9.7-9)⁹

One might believe in seeing yourself in your free whims
Discussing in Cato's fashion virtues and vices,
Deciding the merit and the reward of authors.

As Blackburn would stress, in confusing directive values as perceptible truths, the pedantic classical artist feels justified in condemning any other poet who is incapable of seeing and understanding these values, in dismissing that person as a scribbler of insufficient sensibility and sophistication, as someone who clearly was not born a poet. Yet Boileau is sensible enough to acknowledge that the criteria he imposes on others may simply be the product of his own capricious wit. He displays a noncomplacent honesty when he calls his supposedly inspired judgments into question:

Qui vous a pu souffler une si folle audace ?
Phébus a-t-il pour vous aplani le Parnasse ?

(SAT. 9.23-24)¹⁰

Who was able to breathe into such mad audacity?
Has Phoebus flattened Parnassus for you?

Acts of flattening (*aplanir*) do appear to be prerequisite for the classical goal of pleasing (*plaire*). The abstraction of universal rules, like the bleaching of ancient statuary, was a conscious attempt to smooth out inherited materials for modern accommodation. In its most dogmatic versions, classicism glosses over the effects of time by ignoring any historical perspective or cultural contingency that might qualify the absolutism of its marble-white ideals. They feel compelled to resolve the chromatic dissonance that would disturb delightful reception, failing to recall that in fifth-century Athens whitewashing a work of sculpture was tantamount to a gross deformation, as Euripides's Helen indicates:

τέρας γάρ ὁ βίος καὶ τὰ πράγματ᾽ ἐστί μου,
τὰ μὲν δι᾽ Ἥραν, τὰ δὲ τὸ κάλλος αἴτιον.
εἴθ᾽ ἐξαλειφθεῖσ᾽ ὡς ἄγαλμ᾽ αὖθις πάλιν
αἴσχιον εἶδος ἔλαβον ἀντὶ τοῦ καλοῦ

(EURIPIDES, *HELEN*, 260–63)

My life and deeds are a monstrosity,
in part by Hera, in part my beauty is the cause.
If only, like a statue is plastered back over again,
I could acquire an uglier form instead of a beautiful one

The lines serve as a vivid symbol not only of how the modern taste for some idea of purity conflicted with the polychromatic taste of the ancient Athenians but also of how classicist poets and critics, to some extent, have to be unjust to the past to be just to the present. Yet, should one flatten or neutralize antiquity too extremely, one risks losing the dynamic bifocality, the stereoscopic commitment to both the past and the present that always saves classicism from weak complaisance.

Philology as
Ancilla Facultatum

Classicism is unjust to antiquity insofar as it selects a portion of antiquity to formulate its conceptions and disregards the rest. As Frank Kermode emphasizes, "French classicism in the great century was not ... an artificial imitation of antique models, but an expression of the national mind; the rules it adopted were not antiquarian but rationally French, not old inventions renovated, but nature methodized."[1] Although this methodological achievement resulted from the bifocal labor of negotiating the past and the present, it may tempt idle minds to settle for the convenience of time-tested routine. For the complacent, the prescriptions and criteria are presumed to be fixed in a place that transcends particular works. From a political perspective, such endeavors correspond well with imperial aspirations that attempt to subordinate cultural differences to a transcendent and universalizing entity. In exercising judgment, classical complacency appeals to eternal, universal ideals that are enshrined in a realm that is distinct from ephemerality, mutability, and cultural pluralism. The completeness of the classical past specifically defends it from all time-bound contingencies.

This timeless ideal came to be represented consistently by Rome, the *urbs aeterna* or Eternal City, conceived as an efficacious platform that maintains a perduring identity across historical change. In T. S. Eliot's response to the equally timeless question *What Is a Classic?* Virgil is singled out as the poet who has bestowed European modernity with stable criteria against which subsequent literary initiatives should be assessed. It is this assessment that, according to Eliot, should allow us to recognize what is and is not a classic. He does not intend to proffer Virgil's poetry as a strict model for mere imitation but rather regards this work as transcending the limitations of its own historical moment to a level far beyond what Virgil himself could have possibly foreseen—that is, as a literary ideal that, thanks to a series of unique historical circumstances, was destined to serve as a guiding light in the development of European consciousness and expression. In brief, Virgil's *Aeneid* sets the standard for the maturity and comprehensiveness that Eliot considers to be the very trademark of the classic, not necessarily in terms of specific poetic style but rather in terms of the poem's singular, metahistorical position. Accordingly, as Eliot concludes, "In our several literatures, we have much wealth of which to boast, to which Latin has nothing to compare; but each literature has its greatness, not in isolation, but because of its place in a larger pattern, in a pattern set in Rome."[2]

Although Eliot does not discuss any specific passage from the *Aeneid*, the most compelling model for the metahistorical pattern of which he speaks would be the description of Aeneas's Shield from the eighth book of the epic (8.617–731). Drawing on Homeric and Hesiodic traditions, Virgil's ekphrasis is in itself a masterpiece of classical reception that appropriates ancient sources for present purposes. Yet, in contrast to both Homer's rather pastoral depiction of human community and Hesiod's mythological account of Hēraklēs (Hercules), Virgil provides a comprehensive overview that spans from Rome's archaic foundation, through its long monarchic and republican history, to the triumphant achievement of empire under the aegis of Augustus. From Aeneas's perspective, of course, the entire narrative relates to events still to come. The conceit of futurity reminds the reader that, taken as a whole, the planar surface of the shield flattens the unfolding of time into a single, glorious design.

Still, in the final words of his description, Virgil offers a powerful counterexample by characterizing the River Araxes as *pontem indignatus* (disdaining to bear the bridge; *Aen.* 8.728). After hundreds of lines, the poet concludes this grand symphony, this magnificent union of voices, with this striking coda, sotto voce. The river, today known as the Aras, is named after a royal descendant of the patriarch Haik, who founded the Armenian nation; and the bridge serves as mighty reminder of Roman conquest. As a symbol of ethnic difference and the irrecoverable flow of time, the river is *indignatus*: *indignant* with the bridge that has gathered it into a limitless empire and thus robbed it of its individual *dignity*.

It is the urgent need to preserve the dignity of difference that characterizes the *philological* disposition. Philology reverses classicizing intentions by resisting any gesture that would flatten out or idealize antiquity for the sake of smooth usage and consumption. Philology tends to upset the timeless values that classicism is wont to establish. It has little tolerance for the *lâche complaisance*, or weak complacency, that transmits antiquity through purifying filters. Instead, it adduces the past in all its roughness. As Maurizio Bettini remarks, "[Academics] constantly remind us, in their footnotes and their stylistic and philological analyses, that the classics are *not* modern, but the offspring of a world that is *not* our own and, as such, profoundly *different* from our own."[3]

Traditionally, philology relates to classicism as a servant to a master. Before assuming the highest rank in the nineteenth-century university, and before being dismissed in the latter half of the twentieth century as stuffy, old-fashioned, and self-satisfied, classical philologists had limited themselves to subservient tasks, taking on the menial work that marginalized them from the main academic divisions. Philology worked as the handmaiden to the faculties, as the *ancilla facultatum*.[4] From the perspective of philosophy, medicine, jurisprudence, and theology, philology undoubtedly played a necessary role, particularly regarding the discovery, appraisal, and emendation of manuscripts, as well as the historical-antiquarian research necessary for such textual criticism. Yet this role should ultimately be nonintrusive and deferential. Upon performing the chore of preparing a readable text, philology was to step aside to allow for the more important work of interpretation, including lessons in eternal salvation.

That is not to say that philology itself could not rise to tyrannical levels of power in academic culture, especially when it allied its efforts with scientific and technological methods. Philology, no less than classicism, can settle into a predominantly dogmatic disposition. One thinks of such formidable figures as Richard Bentley, Friedrich August Wolf, August Boeckh, or Ulrich von Wilamowitz-Moellendorff. Yet even these scholars, however staunchly they might have adhered to their views, and however smugly they might have imposed them on others, still had to negotiate with the thoroughly historical principles of their profession.

Philology demonstrated its devotion to classicism as the humble servant to a master discourse. Its painstaking work of collating manuscripts, testing authenticity, and emending texts stemmed from the conviction that it was contributing to a worthwhile enterprise, that its place of employment possessed implicit value. Yet also as a servant, philology risked becoming meddlesome by interrupting the production and communication of knowledge, by pointing out some crux, corruption, or anachronism. Philology prevented easy reading by calling attention to textual problems or by questioning previous emendations. While the professor invited students to partake in a grand feast of words, philology intruded to reset the dishes, noisily and impertinently, disturbing the meal.

Whereas a *faculty* denotes the "ease" (*facilitas*) acquired to absorb and relay knowledge, philology seems to make everything *difficult*, not facile, adhering to the principle *lectio difficilior potior* (the more difficult reading is the stronger). Philology undermines pleasant facility by digging beneath the verbal surface. It refuses to be entirely pleased with the text at hand or thoughtlessly give its placet. While the major faculties aimed to produce definitive results, philologists toiled away ceaselessly. Even at its apex in nineteenth-century German university culture, philology tended to belong to the working class within the academic distribution of labor.

A noncomplacent philology could therefore indulge in blatant acts of insubordination by *displacing* any and all authoritative pronouncements, sometimes in a manner that was wholly *inappropriate* or *déplacée*. In the nineteenth century, philology posed a threat to any classical tradition that required the flattening out of epochal and cultural distinctions. Whereas classicism aimed toward absolutism, philology insisted on relativism. Whereas classicists worked to eliminate historical or cultural qualifications that would compromise the tradition's universal claims, philologists maintained perspectival difference and the historically constructed nature of truths. The tension arguably reaches back to debates between realists and nominalists, scholastics and humanists, to the distinction between philosophy's turn to dialectics and logic for determining the assured knowledge of scientia and philology's reversion to rhetoric and history for indicating the provisional nature of every judgment. The philosopher's scientific *what* contrasted with the philologist's rhetorical *how*.[5]

Despite its obvious connection to humanism, classicism has

always shared, to varying degrees, in philosophy's desire to ascertain some unassailable truth. To accomplish its philosophical mission, classicism must place a moratorium on the multiple semantic trajectories that precede and will continue well beyond verbal definition. It must aim to fix meaning in place and stave off any incursions that would displace it—incursions that philology persistently performed. For philology loved words to such an extent that it refrained from locking any word in a fixed and stable definition. It expressed its loving attachment to words by never ceasing to raise questions, jealously seeking to know more about each word—where it has been, what it has been doing—never allowing any word to rest silently in place. If classicizing initiatives hoped to preserve a sacred precinct of traditional knowledge and continuity, philological activity constituted an invasion from outside the temple, noncomplacent and profane.

To this day, philology may be regarded as profane whenever it takes classical complacency to task by drawing from the hidden depths and metaphorical resources that classic definitions work to suppress. Philology can position itself as questioning the kind of semantic emplacement that makes classicism attractive in the first place—attractive for those who derive pleasure from the pleasing reassurance that everything appears to be exactly where it belongs. The philologist loves words profanely by refusing to hold meaning as sacrosanct and unimpeachable. Powerful institutions that rest on established doctrine must therefore keep philology in check, lest it undermine the basis of their power. As Lorenzo Valla's critique of the Donation of Constantine makes clear, for the philologist, no text is sacred.

For those who take pleasure in keeping traditions in place, philological displacement poses a serious threat. It comes as no surprise, then, that die-hard proponents of the nineteenth-century classical curriculum in England railed against the irruption of rigorous philological approaches, primarily from the German States.[6] Here, philological nitpicking frustrated the communication of sacred, classical ideals. Profane philologists seemed to care more about the use of the ablative absolute or alternative endings of the aorist optative than about the courage of Achilles or the virtue of Cato.

Although by the mid-nineteenth century, classics at the English university had become increasingly professionalized, primarily by adopting the philological-scientific methods of German institutions, the old public school ideal maintained its privileged place in the nation's self-definition. Many men of the ruling class who had benefited from the intensive study of Latin and Greek protested the demise of this hallowed field of higher learning as it began to show signs of fragmentation toward greater specialization, which caused it to drift away from the ideals of a liberal education bent on breeding future gentlemen and civil servants. In 1856, the Cambridge philosopher John Grote complained, "The destruction or disuse of [classical education] will destroy one bond of intellectual communion among civilized men, and will be, in this respect, not a step of improvement."[7] One year later, Lord Houghton voiced a similar lament: "Our lot is cast in the moment of this world's life in which the great instrument of civilization, the Classical Culture, is ceasing to occupy the minds and regulate the intellectual motions of mankind."[8]

Philology's laboriousness boldly contrasted with the nonutilitarian freedom of the elite ruling class. Unlike the educated gentry, philologists relished in getting their hands dirty, burying their noses in the lexica and cluttering their desks with heaps of minutiae. Above all, philology's reliance on other fields—on history and geography, on archaeology and numismatics—had a fracturing effect on the classics. Ever eager to refine its sense of historical perspective or cultural difference, philology appeared to rob the classical curriculum of the timeless truths that once gave classics its uncontested privilege at the highest rank among the disciplines.

The opposition of philology and classicism articulated in the nineteenth century deserves to be revived, especially in light of the recent renaming of the American Philological Association, founded in 1869, as the Society for Classical Studies in 2013. Although this refurbishing arguably aimed to relinquish the label of philology, which never really took root in British academia and long fell into disfavor in the United States as a rather musty, old-fashioned designation, the promotion of classical studies risks suppressing philology's critical force. By emphasizing the fundamentally noncomplacent disposition of philological labor, the old denomination may indeed be reclaimed not simply to speak for intellectual rigor but also to rally against any elitism that one might still ascribe to the term *classics*.

Precisely as an oppositional, thoroughly historicizing disposition, philology can disrupt classicism by attending to the conditions of meaning formation. To produce sense by means of language, to press on with the reading process and understand the message being transmitted, each word encountered must come to rest in some signified content. The problematic nature of words must be handled in some way or other before one can carry on with questioning what those words mean or represent. That said, the philologist seems to understand that any determination can only be provisional, that every page is but a propositional surface, a plank. Even when a text's ideational message is finally conveyed, there remain multiple vectors of meaning and context, hosts of inherent metaphors and images, endless series of connotations and allusions, all of which have historically preceded and will continue to develop beyond the singular act of interpretation. At any given moment, the communicated meaning and its reception are the result of manifold semantic and figurative detours which, despite all cognitive exertion, go on to energize each word and steer them toward new, unforeseen discursive configurations. To believe otherwise is to be lulled into the kind of complacency that sees only textual smoothness with no regard for the furrowed striations that are nonetheless there.

Philology may conduct its investigations either synchronically or diachronically, structurally or historically. One can decide to register, to whatever extent possible, the usage of a term within a clearly demarcated corpus, or one can choose to trace a word's genealogy, how it developed semantically over time, how it accrued modified denotations and left behind others. In this latter case, a diachronic consideration would disturb synchronic usage, if only because it adduces remnants of meaning and context that may evade or even run counter to an author's communicative intention and the recipient's intentional comprehension. While conservative classical discourse may wish to ignore any semiotic noise, philological work positions itself at the crossroads of synchrony and diachrony and allows both axes to revise and alter each other. Philology arrives to upset the conventions that underwrite communication: tacit agreements that bind speakers and listeners, writers and readers, together.

Communication is a contract. It operates with the faith that writers know what they are writing, and readers know what they are reading. Philology, too, works with these linguistic conventions. Yet, like a mad lawyer, the philologist may halt the discursive proceedings by reading the fine print, by citing overlooked clauses or calling in a surprise witness, often to the point where a judgment may be entirely overturned, including any judgment pronounced in the name of philology itself. Classicism's raft of determination is threatened by philological waves of overdetermination. The complacent delusion of safe textual passage runs aground on the shoals of the words employed, implacably.

Philological Investigations

What might a philologically implacable examination of the word *complacency* produce?

Despite its ubiquity in current discourse, the term *complacency* has hardly received any extended examination, neither in the form of philosophical discussion nor by way of semantic scholarship. When complacency is in fact broached—for example, in moral or ethical treatises, in journalism or popular critiques—its definition is almost always presented as self-evident and, on the whole, pejorative. Yet what does this word, precisely as a word, denote? How has its usage across time come to influence the way we employ and think about the concept? What latent figures, what vestigial senses, what hidden or dead metaphors, continue to exert their force whenever the word is pronounced, whenever the notion is evoked? More pointedly expressed: How complacent is our understanding of complacency?

The noun *complacentia* is not extant in classical Latin usage, even though the verbal and adjectival forms—*complacere* and *complacitus*—do appear occasionally in ante- and postclassical sources. At the origins of its semantic career in antiquity, these terms would not immediately evoke the inflated self-satisfaction, idleness, or negligent overconfidence that are connoted today. Rather, constructed from *placere*—the common verb for pleasing and being pleased, for finding something satisfying, agreeable, or acceptable—*complacere* refers to a feeling of contentment with someone or with some state of affairs. The *com-* prefix, a form of the preposition *cum* ("with"), generally introduces a sense of being or bringing together and hence may also denote some idea of completion or perfection. *Complacere* therefore signifies a state of being pleased, further marked by simultaneity or intensification: "to please greatly, to show favor," or "to be pleasing at the same time."

Placere is intransitive, governing a dative object, which tends to emphasize the subjective aspect of the person affected, as in *placet mihi*, "it is pleasing *to me*," "it is pleasing *from my perspective*." In contrast, transitive verbs of pleasing such as *delectare* and *juvare*, in taking an accusative object, accentuate the act of granting pleasure: *te delectat*, "he pleases you," "he delights you," or even "he charms, allures, seduces you"; and *te juvat*, "it pleases you in a helpful or useful way." With these transitive verbs, the predication depends more on the perceived qualities of the person, thing, or event that produces the pleasing effect, while with *placere*, precisely by focusing on the person who judges something to be agreeable, emphasis is on an individual's feelings and experience. This distinction between effect and affect is lost in the English verb *to please*, which is ergative, functioning either transitively or intransitively, denoting both *pleasing someone* as a direct object and *being pleasing to someone* as an indirect object.

The ambivalence does not apply in Latin. As an intransitive verb, *placere* expresses a stated sentiment, belief, or decision. *Placet mihi* may thus signify "it is my opinion," "I hold it to be the case," or "I approve." With reference to a group, the verb can designate a collective resolution, as in the phrase *senatui placet* (the senate decrees)—a proclamation based on senatorial agreement, which persists in modern legal discourse as the noun *placet*, denoting a vote of assent or sanction. Hence, in the perfect tenses, active or passive—*placuit* or *placitum est*—the verb may be translated as "it is decided" or "it is resolved." The substantive *placitum* accordingly denotes not only what is found to be pleasing or acceptable but also, more figuratively, a "determination," a "prescription," and even a "principle" or "maxim."

In early Latin usage, *complacere* maintains the subjective aspect while rendering it more intense. The verb often alludes to a wish to be near someone or a strong desire for personal gratification and reciprocation. An individual's physical appearance is especially pleasing when there is a promise of union, as in Terence: "Her beauty was very pleasing [*complacitam*] to him after he saw her" (*Heaut.* 773). Consequently, one often detects an expression of anxiety over the object of longing, that the awaited pleasure may never be realized. In Terence's *Andria*, Charinus complains to Pamphilus about being caught in a game of mimetic desire involving the girl Philumena; despite their betrothal, Pamphilus has lost interest in Philumena, until Charinus appears on the scene: "After I said I loved her, she's become quite pleasing to you [*complacita'st tibi*]" (*And.* 647).

The yearning for proximity may be colored by the gravest fears as in the Latin translation of Psalm 76, where the singer is deeply troubled by God's current distance—*Numquid in aeternum projiciet Deus? aut non apponet ut complacitior sit adhuc?* (literally translated: "Will God spurn for eternity? Or will he not come near to be *quite favorable* still?" Ps. 76:8 Vulg.).[1] Although the corresponding Hebrew verb *ratsah* simply denotes "to be pleased with, to find acceptable," Jerome's use of *complacitus* in the comparative conveys a greater intensity to reflect the psalmist's nervous desperation. The desire to possess the pleasing entity, the hope for closeness, is driven by the fear that the longed-for pleasure may never arrive.

It is significant that, in the thirteenth century, when Thomas Aquinas introduces the noun *complacentia* into modern vocabulary, he subtracts the element of desire and thereby removes any potential frustration. In Aquinas, *complacentia* implies sheer positivity, a state of complete satisfaction unimpaired by the negativity or lack that instigates yearning. In the Christian tradition, it reflects the loving pleasure that God the Father expressed for his Son: "This is my beloved Son, with whom I am well pleased [*mihi complacui*]" (Matt. 3:17 Vulg.). For the scholastic philosopher, *complacentia* thus emerges in reflections on love (*amor*) and its relationship to the human passions. The question is whether love is the initial motivating cause of our impassioned inclinations or merely a consequent effect of those passions.[2] After disputing a number of authoritative positions that place strong desire (*concupiscentia*) or delightful pleasure (*delectatio*) as antecedent to love, Aquinas appeals to the authority of Augustine, who claims straightforwardly that "all the passions are caused by love."[3] To continue, Aquinas makes further distinctions, again on the basis of Augustine's reflections, specifying *amor* in terms of the two distinct passions that it activates: as the movement of desire (*cupiditas*) and as the attained stillness of joy (*laetitia*).

Aquinas corroborates Augustine's claims by demonstrating that before one moves toward a desired object and finds joyful rest in possessing it, the agent must be positively disposed toward this object and recognize it as something good (*bonum*). Aquinas thus concludes, "This adaptive attachment [*aptitudo*] or matching relation [*proportio*] toward the good is love, which is nothing other than a pleasing disposition toward the good [*complacentia boni*]."[4] Understood, then, as a proportionate affinity with the good, love as *complacentia* is a feeling that underlies and precedes both the movement of concupiscence and the delight of possession—a contemplative, satisfying, and joyful love for what God has granted us, unruffled by any desire for something more.[5]

Elaborating on Aquinas's conception, in his *Treatise on the*

Love of God (1616), Francis de Sales defines *complaisance* as a
mutually balanced love, one "that makes us possessors of God
[*possesseurs de Dieu*], drawing his perfections in us, and makes
us possessed by God [*possédés de Dieu*], attaching us to his perfections."[6] In this Catholic tradition, *complacentia* names a
tranquil gratification with God's creation—a stable attraction,
analogous to Greek *agapē*, an affection that is untroubled by sinful dissatisfaction. *Complacentia* or *complaisance* finds sufficient pleasure with the way things are, undisturbed by negativity; the *not-yet* and the *no-longer* do not tempt the beholder with
lustful concupiscence or transgressive curiosity. Instead, with
complacentia, one is invited to indulge positively in the divine
order of the world. The sheer delight in the status quo, which
characterizes our modern idea of complacency, begins here.

As Aquinas explicitly states, *complacentia* consists of a
fundamental suitability that recalls one of the basic senses of
placere—namely, the notion of agreement between two parties.
Something or someone is found to be agreeable when there
is a felt concordance, when everything appears to be right.
Through the reconciliation of differences, a group establishes
the pleasing conditions for a collective resolution, as already
noted in the classical phrase *senatui placet*. This proclamation
of agreement, however, often remains on the level of appearance, understood as a common accord that masks over the differences between one party and the other. Hence, early modern
lexicographers used the verb *complacere* as a gloss for the Greek
verb *suneudokein*, which denotes giving consent with the implication that the issue "appears" (*dokei*) agreeable to all, that the
resolution is very favorable and well-pleasing (*eudokei*) to both
sides, despite underlying divergences. Agents put aside their
reservations to reach a positive accord; they suppress negative
misgivings for the sake of agreement—a gesture that occurs
merely on the surface of appearances.

All the same, the conciliatory sense of *complacentia* is discernible in the work of Thomas Hobbes, who introduces the word *compleasance* into English to represent what he held to be one of the crucial laws of nature—"that every man strive to accommodate himselfe to the rest" (*Leviathan* [1651], 1.15). Hobbes turns to an architectural figure to illustrate:

> There is in mens aptnesse to Society a diversity of Nature, rising from their diversity of Affections; not unlike to that we see in stones brought together or building of an Aedifice. For as that stone which by the asperity, and irregularity of Figure, takes more room from others, than it selfe fills; and for the hardnesse, cannot be easily made plain, and thereby hindereth the building, is by the builders cast away as unprofitable, and troublesome.[7]

Individuals whose sentiments are aberrant and unyielding resist social integration, just like building stones that are irregular and obdurate. Both "cannot be easily made plain"—in his subsequent Latin translation, Hobbes uses the term *complanari*. Obdurate social types are "unprofitable" and "troublesome" in their recalcitrance, unsuitable for the edification of civil society. As Hobbes concludes this passage on *compleasance*, such difficult individuals are too "stubborn, insociable, froward, intractable" to accommodate themselves with everyone else.

Tellingly, for his Latin translation, Hobbes left out the word *complacentia* and instead simply provided the definition: *ut unusquisque se commodum caeteris praestet* (that every man strive to accommodate himself to the rest). Hobbes perhaps refrains from explicitly employing *complacentia* because the noun is nonclassical, clearly coined by Aquinas and therefore closely bound to the Scholasticism from which he fought to distance himself. For Hobbes, these theological associations presumably do not attend *compleasance*, which is a direct borrowing from the French and simply refers to an appropriate level of civility or a civic desire to please.

For Hobbes, *compleasance* or *complaisance* must be distinguished from the word *complacence*, which came to be linked to dogmatism. *Complacence* entered English vocabulary much earlier, derived from the Latin Scholastics and understood as the passive disposition of being pleased with present circumstances—*complacence* as the English translation of Aquinas's *complacentia boni*. Yet, by the fifteenth century, when the word was first recorded in Middle English, *complacence* already included a sense of vanity or smug erudition, for example, in the translated passage from Thomas à Kempis, cited by the *Oxford English Dictionary*: "Better it is to sauour but a litel wiþ mekenes & litel under stondyng, þan gret tresoures of konnynge wiþ veyn complacence" (*Imitation of Christ*, 3.8 [trans., ca. 1430]). Similarly, in the treatise *Arte & Crafte to knowe well to Dye*, printed by William Caxton in 1490, "complacence" is defined as "vayn glorye."

Hobbes's usage of *complaisance* is free of this negative charge. Indeed, from the mid-seventeenth century onward, *complaisance* describes a positive attitude of civil accommodation, while *complacence* continues to signify either simple contentment or vain self-satisfaction. For Joseph Addison, writing in 1713, *complaisance* names an altogether laudable characteristic that eliminates the negative traits that undermine social cohesion:

> Complaisance renders a superior amiable, an equal agreeable, and an inferior acceptable. It smooths distinction, sweetens conversation, and makes everyone in the company pleased with himself. It produces good-nature and mutual

benevolence, encourages the timorous, soothes the turbu-
lent, humanizes the fierce, and distinguishes a society of
civilized persons from a confusion of savages.[8]

In this regard, complaisance flattens out social hierarchies
and places everyone on equal footing, not unlike the amenable
stones in Hobbes which can be "easily made plain." As Addison
concludes, "In a word, complaisance is a virtue that blends all
orders of men together in a friendly intercourse of words and
actions, and is suited to that equality in human nature, which
everyone ought to consider, so far as is consistent with the order
and economy of the world."[9]

By the mid-eighteenth century, both versions of *complacentia*—passive *complacence* and active *complaisance*—tend to
overlap. As one scholar notes, "'Complaisance' can look like
'complacence' . . . when the desire to please supersedes all other
claims on the judgment, effectively quelling protest or disquiet
about things with which one should be displeased, and 'complacence' can look like 'complaisance' when being well-enough
content obliges—as it frequently does."[10] Thus, *complacency*
comes to signify unwarranted contentment. For clarification,
then, most English authors of the period distinguish justified
complacency, which denotes a state of being pleased when one
ought to be pleased, from the contemptible excessiveness of
self-complacency, which signifies a condition of resting content
when one certainly should not.

In modern French, *complaisance* retains the positive senses
of kindness and a deferential readiness to oblige, while a smug
overestimation of one's own value is denoted with *suffisance*,
which may, however, also be intended to mean justifiable suffi-
ciency. The same holds for Spanish *suficiencia* and Italian *suf-
ficienza*, which may or may not suggest pomposity.

German usage mirrors eighteenth-century English more

closely by marking a distinction between favorable *complacency* and unfavorable *self-complacency*. Thus, obliging "complaisance" translates into *Gefälligkeit*, from the intransitive verb *gefallen* (to please or be pleasing), but is then modified as the pejorative *Selbstgefälligkeit* (self-complacency, vanity). Likewise, legitimate "contentment" or "satisfaction" is expressed by *Zufriedenheit*, in contrast to the deprecatory *Selbstzufriedenheit* (excessive self-satisfaction). This latter pair of terms relates to the kind of "peace" (*Friede*) that subsists within a protected enclosure or precinct (*Einfriedung*), where one is guarded from assaults that would disturb a general sense of tranquility and security. A similar figuration is discernible in the contentment described with the noun *Behagen*, which alludes to the comforting pleasure of finding everything contained within a *Hag*, an area *hedged* off from unpleasant disruptions. In this regard, *Selbstzufriedenheit* can suggest that one's guarded sense of identity has become a self-incurred confinement, limiting the possibilities for expansion and improvement.

As for Latin *complacentia*, philosophers of the eighteenth century upheld a positive notion of appreciative pleasure and concordance, without the stain of vanity that could mar Middle English *complacence*. In his notes on anthropology, Immanuel Kant follows Alexander Gottlieb Baumgarten in relating *complacentia* to the "pleasure" (*voluptas*) of "satisfaction," as opposed to the "displeasure" (*taedium*) associated with "dissatisfaction" (*displicentia*);[11] and subsequently elaborates this usage by translating *complacentia* as *Wohlgefallen* (delight, goodwill, enjoyable appreciation).[12] Similarly, in his collection of published lectures *Anthropology from a Pragmatic Point of View* (1798), Kant describes the formal sense of "taste" as that which "communicates our feeling of pleasure or displeasure to others"—a communication, moreover, that includes the "Wohlgefallen (*complacentia*)" of sharing one's opinion "communally [*gemeinschaftlich*]" with others.[13] *Complacentia* thus serves as the very glue that binds communities together: a mutual disposition that brings individuals together in concordance. On the level of verbal form, Kant's translation of *complacentia* as *Wohlgefallen* underscores the communally beneficial attributes of obliging *complaisance* (*Gefälligkeit*) by supplanting the private "self" (*Selbst*) of egocentric, vain *complacence* (*Selbstgefälligkeit*). This move is, in the end, not unrelated to Hobbes's ideal of *compleasance* as a manner of accommodation and social cohesion, whereby each individual allows the diversity of his or her "affections" to "be easily made plain"—*complanari*—like the smoothened stones that constitute the edifice of civil society.

Pleasingly Flat

In likening a complaisant citizen to a stone "easily made plain"—in linking *complacentia* with the verb *complanari*—Thomas Hobbes's text can be read as engaging in an etymological figure that provocatively connects *placere* with *planus*.

Without the benefit of our current linguistic methods for reconstructing Indo-European roots, writers from antiquity to early modernity have employed the homophonic, formal sequence *pla-* to make implicit etymological arguments that relate Latin *placere* to the Greek noun *plax*, *plakos* (anything flat or broad, particularly a flatland or plain) as well as to the Greek adjective *platus* (flat, wide, broad) and its Latin synonym *planus*.[1] The *pla-* sequence therefore acquired a nearly morphemic character, which would suggest that a perception of smoothness or evenness underlies the pleasing affect expressed specifically by *placere*—walking across a pleasantly level ground free of uneven patches; gazing out onto the calm surface of the sea, without the threat of rough waters; or gliding one's hand along a smooth surface uninterrupted by distracting bumps or blemishes. In these and analogous cases it makes sense to define the pleasant experience with a determining negation (free of, without, uninterrupted), as if the feeling of being pleased is somehow resultative, as if one is especially pleased when expected disturbances fail to occur or have been successfully removed. The same would appear to apply to perceptions of internal states: a feeling of tranquility, no longer in thrall to upsetting passions or disruptive impulses; or finding a solution to a nagging problem. The sense of accommodation that Hobbes hears in the term *compleasance* clearly belongs to this experience of smooth transactions and congenial collaboration, where the potential disruption of different opinions and aims has been leveled out into common accord.

The folk-etymological link to flatness and evenness could be employed to distinguish *placere* from other Latin terms denoting pleasant emotional responses. At times, these adjectives exhibit true etymological derivations, which arguably contribute to each word's semantic depth, even if these substrates of meaning escaped a writer's notice. *Gratus* describes that which is pleasing in a loving or thankful fashion—in a manner that shows *gratitude* for favors bestowed. The nominal form *gratia* refers to mutual esteem or kindly regard and was often understood as a synonym for Greek *charis* (grace) and *charma* (source of joy, delight), which are cognate with Sanskrit *haryāmi* (take pleasure) as well as Latin *horior* (encourage, urge) and *hortus* (pleasure garden). The root here has been reconstructed as *$\acute{g}^her$–, which gives us German *gern* (gladly, willingly) and English *yearn*.

Somewhat distinct from *gratus*, a delightfully charming and inviting place can be characterized as *amoenus*, which may evoke the Greek adjective *ameinōn*, "better," the comparative form of *agathos*, "good." Moreover, within the Latin context, the formal appearance of *amoenus* could conjure notions of "love" (*amor*) and "friendship" (*amicitia*). The list can certainly be expanded. Something may be "pleasing" when it is "wished for or welcome" (*optatus*) or "accepted" (*acceptatus*), or when it causes delight in a playful manner (*iucundus*, heard as related to *iocus*, "joke"). A pleased affect attends fruitful enjoyment (*fruens*) or a joyful outcome (*gaudens*); just as there is pleasure in whatever occasions cheerfulness (*laetus* < Indo-European *pri-, another term for "love," which subsists in Greek *praos*, "mild, gentle," German *Friede*, "peace" and *Freude*, "joy," and English *free*).

In a letter written to his father's personal secretary Tiro (44 BCE), young Marcus Cicero has recourse to this entire vocabulary of pleasantness to express or feign relief, while studying abroad in the seductively entertaining city of Athens:

> After I had been eagerly awaiting the letter-carriers daily, they finally arrived forty-six days after they had left you. The arrival of which was most welcome [*exoptatissimus*]; for although I took the greatest pleasure [*laetitiam*] in the letter from my kindest and dearest father, still your most delightful [*iucundissimae*] letter truly brought for me the culminating point of joy [*gaudi*]. And so, I am no longer sorry for having stopped writing but rather I was cheerful [*laetabar*]; for I received great enjoyment [*fructum*] from silencing my correspondence, and I therefore rejoice [*gaudeo*] exceedingly that you have accepted [*accepisse*] my excuse without hesitation. That the rumors conveyed about me are pleasing and welcome to you [*gratos tibi optatosque*], I do not doubt, my dearest Tiro. (*Fam.* 16.21.1)

These expressions of personal pleasure, sincere or otherwise, stem from the relief Marcus feels after learning that his father remains favorably disposed toward him. The letter has assured him that his behavior is being reported in a way that his father would wish for (*optatos*), in a way that exhibits filial gratitude (*gratos*). Marcus goes on to describe how he "pleasurably" (*libenter*) listens to his teacher Cratippos, cherishing the older man's "pleasantness" (*suavitatem*; *Fam.* 16.21.3)—that is, the philosopher's lectures spark desire (*libenter* < *libet*, "it is pleasing or desirable," cognate with German *Liebe*, "love," and *Lob*, "praise"); his manner is pleasant in a way that is almost "sweet" to the taste (*suavis*, related to the Greek *hēdus* and *hēdonē*). He adores "the most delightful company" (*iucundissima convictio*) of his teacher Bruttius, who does not take the "fun" (*iocus*) out of philological discussions (*Fam.* 16.21.4). Altogether, the feeling of exculpation, the assurance of his good reputation, and the sheer delight of his lessons are indeed very pleasing to him. And yet, the ingratiating young man never says *placet mihi*.

Placere has more to do with finding a common ground of agreement, where nothing bothersome stands in the way. From the same book of letters to Tiro, Cicero the father writes from the home of his host Xenomenes in Leucas, expressing his wish to have his beloved secretary be taken there, where he might complete his cure: "It was pleasing to me [*mihi placebat*], if you are feeling stronger, that he [Xenomenes] might bring you to Leucas, where you could regain your strength entirely [*plane*]" (*Fam.* 16.21.5). The passage not only expresses an agreement reached between the speaker and his host (*mihi placebat*), but also because it promises a cure that would be accomplished "entirely" (*plane*). The etymological figure, whether or not intentional, underscores clearance in both cases: the absence of dispute between Cicero and Xenomenes correlates to the absence of any obstruction that would prevent Tiro from complete recovery. The path is marked "clearly"—*plane*—at each stage. To be sure, Marcus Cicero's description of joy and cheerfulness in the letter quoted earlier also implies the alleviation of some pain: the elimination of guilt for not having written sooner, the eradication of doubt that he might be perceived as immoral, the removal of tedium in his daily lessons. Yet these kinds of results differ, however slightly, from the satisfying arrangement of a viable *plan*, where everything has fallen neatly into place, without hindrances.

In his *Panegyric to Trajan*, delivered a century and a half later in 100 CE, Pliny the Younger employs nearly the same figure when he describes the general's return to Rome to ascend the throne of emperor. Having just assumed the office of suffect consul, Pliny is eager to inspire the consensus that would ensure political stability. He therefore takes the solemn occasion of addressing the Senate to emphasize Trajan's refreshing policies: his appeal to traditional mores, his benevolence to the people, and not least of all, his conformity with the will of the patricians. With oratorical finesse, Pliny praises the ruler's military accomplishments abroad and his effective governance at home—achievements that shine all the more brilliantly when compared with the dark and vicious reigns of previous tyrants such as Nero and Domitian. Although the state remains under autocratic rule, the former general and optimal prince will allow liberty to flourish. It is at this point that Pliny recounts the general's triumphant return to the capital almost three years before:

> Now the desires of the citizens were calling you back, and esteem for your country exceeded your love for the army camp. The road thence [was] placid [*iter inde placidum*] and gentle, plainly [*plane*] belonging to someone returning from a settled peace. (*Paneg.* 20.1)

As in the Cicero passage, *placere*—here in the adjectival form *placidus*—occurs in proximity with the adverb *plane*. With this figure, Pliny links the former life of military campaigns in foreign lands with the present imperial office at Rome, a continuity symbolized by the "peaceful road" (*iter placidum*) that leads from one realm to the next and correlates the emperor's "love for the army camp" to his "esteem for his country." Trajan's philanthropic rule, the principal theme of Pliny's encomium, is thereby established. Yet, as in every notable rhetorical exercise, the parallels between securing an accord in Germania and exercising moderate governance in Rome cannot be limited to the level of narrative. Rather, the syntax and the particular word choices aim to convey the message persuasively. The alliterative rhyme of *placidus* and *plane* speaks to this intention.

Likewise, the paved route into the city is described in a nominal sentence—that is, without a finite verb, hence the brackets in my translation: "The road thence [was] placid and gentle." Insofar as a conjugated verb expresses person, tense, and aspect, the absence of a verbal component could suggest a lack of temporal and aspectual qualifications, an omission of subjective perspective.[2] By eliding a finite verb, Pliny's nominal sentence could come across as a bare assertion of fact, unrestricted by contingencies or personal opinion. It is "plainly" the case and not the result of situational conditions or partisan bias. By not including a verbal marker, the road that joins military service and civic leadership is portrayed as a symbol of stability immune to change or contrariety. Already at the head of his speech, Pliny promised that his "act of thanksgiving would be as far removed from a semblance of mere adulation as it is from constraint" (*Paneg.* 1.6). The nominal description of Trajan's path to the Forum is a telling example of the orator's efforts to downplay subjective sentiments or any external pressure. It is *plainly* there for all to see.

The notion of clarity conveyed by *planus* refers to things being laid out flat in the open, without obstructions, illustrated by an evenly paved road. The description of Trajan's placid transition planes all qualifying distinctions, not only the distinctions of individual perspective but also those that obtain in the differences between past, present, and future. The emperor's benevolence is portrayed as an unquestionable verity, immune to any changes or modifications that would come with the unfolding of time or a shift in subjective perspective. Pliny appears to expect that his audience will glide across his plain-dealing discourse and unhesitatingly utter a senatorial *placet*.

Eager to win agreement, before publishing his panegyric, Pliny solicited the advice of his friend Voconius Romanus, an accomplished, asking if he "would consider the beauty [*pulchritudinem*] as well as the difficulty [*difficultatem*] of its theme" and mark which portions "are pleasing" (*placere*) and which ones "have displeased" (*displicuisse*; *Epist.* 3.13). Although the latter pair of criteria form an opposition, the former pair reveal mutual implication; as Pliny explains, the *beauty* of his subject matter is also the source of its *difficulty*. The theme of the emperor's praiseworthiness is already familiar and acceptable to everyone: it is "a matter of common knowledge that has all been said before." This is precisely what makes his theme beautiful (*pulcher*), which means generally satisfying, unlike "novel topics" (*novitas*), which elicit keen scrutiny of the message in order to judge its veracity. The problem for the writer is that beautiful themes that already enjoy consensus cause the reader to become "idle and unconcerned" (*otiosus securusque*); and, in accepting the truth of the topic, the reader pays closer attention to diction and style—that is, to artistic qualities with which satisfaction is more difficult to achieve. When readers already agree with the message, they glide over the content and instead focus on formal features, which require greater effort on the part of the author. Pliny knows that the content of his speech will be broadly pleasing—*placens*—and therefore asks his discerning friend to indicate anything that comes across as stylistically displeasing.

A work that is "beautiful" (*pulcher*) is one that pleases the audience or readership. It is accepted without reservations, untarnished by any objections. For this reason, *pulcher* can be interpreted figuratively as morally "excellent," "noble," or "honorable." Alliteration, again, together with metathesis, forms a subtle connection between *pulcher* and *placere*, two terms that certainly share a number of semantic features.[3] The Lewis and Short Oxford Latin dictionary in fact suggests a kinship between *pulcher* and *parere* (to come forth and be visible), which recalls the visual clarity expressed by the adverb *plane*. Moreover, *parere* may be related to the adjective *par* (equal, matching) and the verbs *polire* (to smooth, to polish) and *parare* (to even out that which is uneven), which are nearly synonymous with the smoothness and evenness expressed by *planus*. Something *appears* beautiful when every component is well situated, when all tensions or contradictions have been compositionally resolved—when everything strikes the observer as plainly pleasing. Aquinas makes an implicit appeal to etymological verification when he defines "beautiful things" as "those which are pleasing to the eye"—*pulchra sunt quae visa placent* (*Summ. Theol.* pt. 1, quest. 5, art. 4)—a tag that James Joyce selected as a core principle of his protagonist's aesthetic theory.[4]

The image of laying something flat in the open, of making everything perfectly visible, motivates the accord expressed by *placere*. In the languages of the Tocharians, a people who occupied the Far Eastern Tarim Basin during the early medieval period, the related terms *plākäm* and *plāki* refer to the agreement reached by opposing groups who approach each other to put aside all differences. The reconciliation presumably rests on finding a common place upon which former hostilities may be forgotten, a place of amnesty, based on terms pleasing to both sides.

The charge of conformism often leveled against the complacent subsists in the Latin cognate *placare* (to soothe, to assuage, to appease, to *placate*), which expresses the desire to resolve disputes. Homophony, again, might suggest a relationship to the verb *plicare* (to fold or wind together), *supplicare* (to bend the knee, supplicate), and Greek *plekein* (to plait, to twine). The connection is justifiable insofar as it portrays the agreement in *placere* as a capacity to bend to the will of another, to be—as Hobbes suggests—amenable, accommodating, *complaisant*. This sense of flexibility may be further detectable in the Greek cognate *plattein/plassein* (to form or mold), as in the nouns *plasma* and *plaster*.

The flatness described by *planus* is heard in many Latin cognates—for example, *palma* (the flat *palm* of the hand), *plancus* (flat-footed), and the postclassical noun *planca* (board, plank). Related terms include German *Feld* (field) as a flattened area of ground, similar to the English *plain* as a flat, level field in the country and *plane* as any flat surface. English *plate*, as well as German *platt* (flat, dull), derives via medieval Latin, from Greek *platus*, while *flat* comes from Proto-Germanic **flata-*, which may represent an extension of the root **pleh₂-* that gives us *planus*. German *flach* (flat, shallow, level) and *Fläche* (surface), including *oberflächlich* (superficial), reach back to Proto-Germanic **flaka-*, which may also be regarded as some obscurely formed elaboration of **pleh₂-*. In addition, there is Old Norse *flō* (layer, coating) as in English *floe*, a "flat sheet of floating ice," Old English *flōc* (flatfish, *fluke*), and Middle English *flake* (thin piece of material peeled off a larger object).

These etymological reflections call attention to metaphors of flatness that persist as vestiges of former lifeworlds, traces of signification that are all but concealed in our modern conceptual vocabulary.[5] The latent images could either confirm or undermine the subject's discursive mastery. In any event, for the sake of convenience and smooth communication, speakers must limit such attentiveness, dealing with words instead as if they were mere slips of paper on which a clear signification is inscribed.

Platea

The history of how philosophy gave precedence to the generalities of *space* over the idiosyncrasies of *place* has been well documented.[1] Despite complications, one can discern a trajectory of thought that stretches more or less continuously from the fifth century BCE to the European Enlightenment: a metaphysical itinerary that exhibits increasingly greater abstraction.

It was the atomists, Leucippus and Democritus, who first mapped out the speculative flight from bounded locality to unbounded immensity. Their central theory of the "void" would conflict with Aristotle's insistence on grounded, inhabited topoi. For Aristotle, every place is an occupied place; and whereas his model of emplacement as confinement may support a human wish for protective shelter and warm embrace, an atomist cosmology based on empty space (*to kenon*) would respond to the converse longing for nonconfinement and liberation from containment. Subsequently, with Neoplatonic theory attendant, the journey toward empty space would be further fueled by medieval theology, which needed to find cosmic room for God's ubiquity. After the advent of new science, the persistent turn away from concrete locations was abetted by purely mathematical accounts of natural phenomena. Elegant numerical demonstrations cared little for the scrappiness of the genius loci. In this regard Christianity and secular Science proceeded in concert: both are universal in their aspirations; both give abstract space the upper hand. Evacuated of all intrinsic qualities, place had dissolved into space, at least in terms of philosophical reflection. One would have to wait for post-Enlightenment thought, for phenomenology and fundamental ontology, before discovering a renewed place for place.

This overarching narrative of how *place* suffered negligence in the history of speculation constitutes a key feature of Western metaphysics. It is the path of every theoretical position that aims to distance itself from the trees of particular differences for the forest of general classification. The itinerary marked here, itself a product of gross generalization, is one that travels toward purified spatiality and a concomitant impoverishment of emplacement, toward universally applicable quantification and the marginalization of sensory, experiential qualifications.

A second theme supplements this primary narrative, an important subplot—namely, the story of how *place* became *flat*. As philosophical reflection displaced notions of place in favor of space, place itself became flattened. As the bounded particularity of three-dimensional locations was being disregarded by European geometrism—abandoned in favor of abstract, universal *spatium*—vernacular conceptions of place underwent a critical leveling, with the result that, when questions concerning emplacement reemerged as topics of philosophical interest, they would bear a modern sense of flatness that ancient proponents of place had engaged.

Although Greek *topos* and Latin *locus* can rightfully be translated as *place*, this translation obscures the notion of flatness inherent in the source-term *plateia*. Ancient conceptions of *topos*, as well as of *locus*, explicitly and consistently refer to three-dimensional space. Both Plato's *Timaeus* and Aristotle's *Physics*, the two most authoritative texts on questions of spatiality, take *topos* to be volumetric. In Plato's likely story, a *topos* is an accommodating place carved out from amorphous unlimited space (*chōra*) and configured by the elemental bodies that occupy it; a *topos* has volume because it contains a solid shape, for "the form of a body in every case also has depth [*bathos*]" (*Tim.* 53c). Similarly, according to Aristotle, a material body fits tightly in its place; they belong to each other, even as bodies move from one place to the next. Aristotle therefore conceives of *topos* as constituted by multiple planes, "some surface [*epipedon*] that is both like a vessel and an embracing thing" (*Phys.* 212a28–29). Regarded either as the limiting edge (*peras*) of the contained body or as the boundary (*horos*) that belongs to the container, a place acquires its shape from the shape it envelops. Its multiple surfaces are coextensive with the same number of parameters that comprise physical entities. As Aristotle bluntly declares, "In fact a *topos* has three extensions: length, breadth, and depth" (*Phys.* 209a5).

Whereas *topos* could readily be employed in geometric reflections, the rarer term *plateia* had a more concrete signification. Like the four major roads excavated at Thurii, *plateiai* were hard-packed surfaces, beaten flat. Ranging from fourteen to thirty meters across, these main arteries gave clear definition to the city's plan. In his historical report on the region, Diodorus writes:

> The Athenian colonists divided the city lengthwise into four streets . . . and breadthwise they divided it into three streets [*plateias*]. . . . And since the passages were filled with dwellings, the city appeared to be well constructed. (Diod., *Lib.* 12.10.7)

The description makes clear that the *plateiai* are seen as planar surfaces, composed only of "length" (*mēkos*) and "breadth" (*platos*)—that is, without the "depth" (*bathos*) that subsists in conceptions of *topos*.

This absence of depth, however, should hardly be regarded as an impoverishment. On the contrary, pure flatness could connote firmness, directness, and strength, reminiscent of the "flat blade" (*platē*) of an oar that cuts through and against the waves, or the "broad oath" (*platus orkos*) that, according to Empedocles, seals the "oracle of necessity" and regulates the cosmic cycle of love and strife (*Emp.* 30.3). Such broad power can also be aimed derisively, as in Aristophanes's *Peace*, where the comic poet summons the Muses to cast a "wide [*platu*] spray of spit" upon the tragic poet Melanthius and his brother (*Pax*, 815). Along similar lines, the comic eye observes the broad, incisive smile of the one who jeers.

Philosophy's most famous nickname further illustrates the power of flatness. Diogenes Laertius records at least three possible reasons for how the name *Plato* (*Platōn*) was given: some claim it was the young man's wrestling coach who first assigned the sobriquet, alluding to the boy's "robust health"; while others refer to the thinker's "broad or extensive manner [*platutēta*] of interpretation"; and others still to his " flat [*platus*] forehead" (*Diog. Laert.* 3.1). The moniker may therefore evoke the philosopher's brute power, his tireless and compelling argumentation, the blatant force of his commanding visage—all of which were capable of striking down opponents as if with the "palm" (*plateia*) of his hand. In this regard, Plato resembles his teacher Socrates, who was long reputed of bewitching and benumbing his interlocutors, like a "flat [*plateiai*] sea-ray" (*Meno* 80a).

In designating a broad thoroughfare within the city, *plateia* transmits some of this extensive power, particularly as a place of public gathering. It is where people go to see and be seen, hear and be heard. Thus, Pindar describes the major streets of Aigina:

πλατεῖαι πάντοθεν λογίοισιν ἐντι πρόσοδι
νᾶσον εὐκλέα τάνδε κοσμεῖν.

(*NEM.* 6.47–48)

There are broad avenues [*plateiai*] going all around for the elo-
  quent ones
to adorn this famous island.

A broad and flattened *plateia* facilitates broadcasting and
thereby functions as a potent medium for communicating the
glory of the city's founders and its citizens. The choral lyric of
Pindar's *epinikia* is capable of traveling conveniently along the
cleared paths that connect one district to the next, again, similar to the *iter placidum* paved by Pliny's oratory. The praise is
unstinting because its path is wide, not narrow. Such a communal location may also become a site of public mourning or
even military engagement—for example, when Dion of Syra-
cuse brazenly greets the enemy, marching "through blood and
fire and the mass of dead bodies lying in the streets [*plateiais*]"
(Plutarch, *Dio*. 46). Above all, the *plateia* served as an ostenta-
tious thoroughfare or *Prunkstraße* representing a city's prosperity, prestige, and ambitions—for example, in Antioch, where
the main boulevard was flanked with grand colonnades, or in
Alexandria, where the *plateia* was bordered by monumental
porticoes.[2]

  Platea enters Latin around the second century BCE, presumably under the influence of increased commerce with Hel-
lenic culture.[3] As a loanword, the term is somewhat rare in classical Latin, which tends to use *via* to denote any major artery
through the urban center.[4] Still, when *platea* is used (e.g., in
Plautus and Terence), it retains the Greek sense of a wide ave-
nue where townspeople live, travel, and gather:

Naucratem quem convenire volui, in navi non erat,
necque domi neque in urbe invenio quemquam qui illum viderit.
Nam omnis plateas perreptavi, gymnasia et myropolia . . .
(PLAUTUS, *AMPHITRYON*, 1009–11)

Naucrates, whom I wanted to meet, was not on a ship,
neither at home nor in the city can I find anyone who might have
    seen him.
For I crawled through all the streets, the gymnasia and the per-
    fumer's shops . . .

Unlike *via*, the *platea* is always found within a city's limits as a
site of busy activity, which its breadth and length allow. It is the
place on which characters stand and mingle. It is where figures
catch one's eye and where events begin to unfold:

sed quis hic est, qui in plateam ingreditur
cum novo ornatu specieque simul?
pol quamquam domi cupio, opperiar,
quam hic rem agat animum advortam.

(PLAUTUS, *TRINUMMUS*, 4.1.21-24)

But who is this, who's entering the street
With new garb and a new look as well?
Indeed, though I want to be at home, I'll wait around,
And pay attention to what this guy is doing.

    Catullus, who uses the word only once in the extant poems,
stresses the bustling atmosphere of the *platea*. In *Carmina* 15, the
speaker entrusts a young boy to his friend Aurelius with the hope
that the youth be preserved for the poet's own erotic pleasure:

non dico a populo: nihil veremur
istos qui in platea modo huc modo illuc
in re praetereunt sua occupati
verum a te metuo

(*CARM*. 15.6-9)

I'm not saying from the people: I do not fear
those who pass by on the street here and there
occupied with their own business—
in truth I fear you

Here, the *platea* portrays a scene of commotion, with anony-
mous people (*istos*) flitting about in every direction. In Catullus's poem, the speaker finds his friend's private quarters to be
the site of the real threat, as opposed to the open space of the
city street—an assessment that distinguishes between a *locus*
with hidden depths and the *platea* that is nothing but surface,
completely exposed to public view. The open *platea* is therefore
safer in comparison with the interior of Aurelius's home. One
could say that the menace resides in the residence itself—in the
domestic *locus* that contains and confines the body within. The
violence that Aurelius might exercise on the boy may indeed be
linked to a reserve of hidden power, a formidable threat that is
concealed behind the façade facing the street. Asymmetrical
relationships of power always depend upon some kind of secret
reserve, which the stronger have over the weaker. Catullus fears
what remains inaccessible to him—the dark dwelling to which
he is entrusting his beloved. Even the thought of the boy entering this interior sets the poet's imagination loose. In contrast,
the *platea* is comforting—pleasing, because it is all surface, a
site of transparency, an even field where people go about their
quotidian lives. Even though, admittedly, many of these Roman
citizens harbor secret passions and violent designs, the flatness
of the street produces a leveling effect that the poet finds reassuring.

The surface of the city thoroughfare may leave someone less
vulnerable to insidious intent, yet the lack of depth can also
jeopardize creative reflection, as in Horace's *Epistle* 2.2:

"purae sunt plateae, nihil ut meditantibus obstet."
Festinat calidus mulis gerulisque redemptor,
torquet nunc lapidem, nunc ingens machina tignum,
tristia robustis luctantur funera plaustris,
hac rabiosa fugit canis, hac lutulenta ruit sus:
i nunc et versus tecum meditare canoros.
Scriptorum chorus omnis amat nemus et fugit urbem.

(*EPIST*. 2.2.71-77)

"The *plateae* are clean, nothing to stand in the way of thinking."
An ardent builder rushes by with mules and workers,
A giant machine brandishes a boulder and then a beam,
Sad funerals wrestle with oakwood wagons,
A rabid dog is fleeing here, a muddied sow rushes there:
Now go and meditate on melodious verses!
The entire chorus of writers loves the grove and flees the city.

The surface noise that spreads across the busy *plateae* flattens the mind and robs the poet of that internal depth where meditation flourishes. Potential melodies are drowned out in the prose of the world.

A *place* may be pleasing because it furnishes a level ground that is traversable without the problems or *problēmata* that would otherwise be "cast before" us (*probeblēmena*), jutting up from the flat land and thus menacing our sure-footed path. By extension, a *plan* attempts to put imminent events into an order and thereby keep them in place, eliminating problematic contingencies, flattening out the future into a smooth itinerary that one believes will proceed without turbulence. Today's sense of complacency may retain the conviction that the course of one's life is already laid out, to be read on the *palm* of one's hand.

The complacent are pleased with having found their *place* in the world, satisfied in knowing that everything rests firmly in its assigned location. In this regard, any true change would represent a displeasing displacement. For the complacent person, a plan once established is the plan that should remain in place, without alteration or revision. Complacency therefore spells a failure to recognize the potential benefit of difficulties. By adhering to the status quo, by maintaining an even keel, complacency underestimates the value of the new. For those who are already successful and prosperous, for those who believe they have arrived at the very summit of well-being, change can only mean a catastrophic turn. Complacency dissuades us from admitting that taking an unexpected detour or entering upon an unfamiliar route may turn out to be a profitable opportunity. As a result, complacency leaves us on a *plateau* with nowhere else to go.

The War on Complacency

What I hate more than anything is complacency and vulgarity.

JACQUES DERRIDA, INTERVIEW BY OSVALDO MUÑOZ

Complacency has little place in an age bent on moving forward. In societies driven by innovation and advancement, being excessively self-content or accepting the status quo is disdained as going against basic beliefs about what human life is or ought to be. Remaining absolutely sated, complacent individuals refrain from making any further efforts. They are happy to do nothing further even though there is clearly so much to be done, convinced that they can glide smoothly through existence without changing course. With ostensibly classical contentment, they nestle into the security and comfort of what they know and thereby cripple growth and development, smothering the will with deadening acquiescence.

Today, the complacent are impugned as society's sleepwalkers, blamed for sloppy misjudgments and insufficient action. They are accused of allowing catastrophes to happen because a disproportionate trust in standard procedures has rendered them incapable of predicting any threat that falls beyond established frames of reference. Physicians, surgeons, and medical staff run the risk of malpractice when they rely too much on past experience, when they see only what they expect to see, misapprehending the specific nature of a patient's symptoms or fatally rejecting the advice of others. Complacent officials, managers, and administrators put too much faith in protocol and thereby overlook problems in their operations. Security personnel and intelligence analysts are derelict when they fail to connect the dots. Scholars and teachers who settle for routine allow their talents to wither away into unproductive careers, ultimately proving themselves to be out of touch, less effective, and less relevant. Science languishes when it remains wholly satisfied with conventional models and presuppositions.

For individuals who are perfectly delighted with themselves and the way things stand, any radical change would only be perceived as a disturbing development. For them, it is much more pleasing to abide with what is expected, to go on doing the same as always. Still, the idleness associated with complacency should not be confused with the utter inaction of resignation. The complacent person still acts, even though this activity aims to keep everything as it currently is or has been. The key distinction involves a difference in temporal orientation: whereas complacency attends pleasurably to the past, resignation looks bleakly onto the future. The resigned person ceases to act under the belief that subsequent action would be futile, while the complacent person performs the way he or she has always performed, operating with the conviction that previous methods are flawless and sufficient.[1] With resignation, there is *nothing more* to do because any hope for future success has been deemed impossible. In contrast, with complacency, there is *nothing new* to do because everything needed for ongoing success is already at hand.

The classical presumption (*nothing new*) may balk at resigned conclusions (*nothing more*), yet from the modernist perspective, complacent routine always risks falling into the trap of idle apathy. The modernist fight is committed to the *new* for the sake achieving *more*—an implacable will to forgo any past construed as a restrictive blueprint in order to actualize an improvable future. Interminably restless, modernity represents a Faustian age, which finds the stores of knowledge set in heavy volumes to be dissatisfying, oppressive, and debilitating. Standardized planning and rote responses are for the weak-willed. In the beginning was the Deed, not the Word!

Modern implacability expresses the sentiment that the world is not as it should be, that change is vitally necessary, on a personal and social level. Accordingly, mobility, novelty, and risk-taking receive far more admiration than sluggishness, habit, and safe bets. We applaud the doers and the fighters, the trailblazers and the rising stars. We praise those who identify systemic deficiencies, atrocious inadequacies, or flagrant injustices and diligently work to correct them. We glorify those who pull themselves out of serious ruts and successfully reinvent themselves. They are the ones who deserve our recognition; they are the ones who should be emulated; while slackers, cowards, and quitters are to be pitied, if not outright vilified. One must constantly be on guard against becoming too content with past achievements. One must always bear in mind that dissatisfaction is prerequisite for achieving something better, that one should never look back and never give up, that being pleased is the surest way of staying forever in place.

The current war on complacency unifies portions of the population that are otherwise at odds with each other. In the realm of business and finance, fervid entrepreneurs know that they can never rest on prior victories, that becoming lackadaisical can only mean watching others race ahead. The fast-paced, nonstop global marketplace demands incessant alertness and insatiable ambition, lest a precious opportunity pass by. Venturesome speculators understand how outdated thinking thwarts growth and undercuts profitability. One has to acknowledge how the rate and volume of transactions has increased beyond all traditional measure, how one's competitors can always gain the cutting edge. Sudden fluctuations, divergent parameters, and abrupt contingencies call for indefatigable alertness. "Classical" paradigms are to be overturned. Acquiring new skills and adopting inventive strategies are the only certain means for continued success.

From a different angle, now in regard to social engagement and activism, remaining content in a civilization that should breed discontent is rebuked for overlooking the facts, hiding from reality, and thus blocking a better future. If complacency jeopardizes profit margins in the realm of commerce and trade, it menaces the common good in the world at large. Choosing to repose in the face of grievous conditions signals a frightening lapse in attentiveness. Lying flat instead of rising up in angry protest represents a cowardly surrender, a renunciation of one's civic duty. In politics, complacency is regarded as an insidious trap that leads one to misjudge the potency and efficacy of opposing parties. Comfort relaxes vigilance and thereby creates an ideological vacuum that other voices are ready to fill. The recent rise of populist and nationalist tendencies, both in the United States and in Europe, has shown all too well how the complacency of a liberal intelligentsia underestimated atavistic tensions that had been festering beneath the surface for quite some time.

For the radical Left, which decries global colonialism, letting things continue as usual amounts to a loathsome moral failure. For zealous dissidents who denounce the merciless objectives of corporatism and capitalism, complacency is indicted as a grave crime, particularly in face of such insatiable rapacity and exploitation. Long-standing policies must be dismantled. People must be roused from apathy and obsequious indifference. One is called upon to reverse the trends that bleed the earth of its resources and threaten environmental disasters. The by now habitual clamor against powerful symbols of world leadership unleash rising levels of violence, if only to show the world that at least a part of the population is not willing to stand by passively. Outraged displays are deemed necessary, if not to end once and for all the many abuses of power—the global corruption, the gross injustices, the flagrant profiteering—then at least to expose the excessive violence of the system itself.

Right-wing populism and nationalism, especially in its extremist forms—hate groups, conspiracy theorists—are equally loath to remain complacent, eager to battle a system they regard as corrupt. They feel called upon to make a stand against what they perceive to be powerful, inimical forces. With implacable fervor, they believe they are peering beneath the sheen of propaganda, discerning insidious motives at work in the depths of public institutions and media.

An aversion to complacency is therefore discernible in all walks of life, regardless of political affiliation, social class, or cultural orientation. Whether in campaigning for a particular party or mobilizing mass protests, whether in organizing community services or competing on the floor of the stock exchange, whether in improving one's career, advancing one's profession, or struggling against sterile conventionalism in the arts—all express hostility toward sitting still and always doing the same.

Once complacency sets in, it proves difficult to extricate oneself, if only because it would imply a move toward something displeasing. It becomes arduous, if not altogether painful, to detach oneself from the comfort zone. Hypnotized by the appeal of what is pleasing, one becomes paralyzed, trapped within the dictates of a distinctly nonerotic pleasure principle, one that is perhaps complicit with a drive toward deathly inertia.

To remain passively content with circumstances that beg for change can only be perceived as unheroic and shameful, a weak gesture that succumbs to comfort. Protest must be mounted against the ancien régime that wishes for nothing less than keeping every citizen in place. As implacable spirits know, this manner of emplacement is detrimental both to individuals and to society at large, for it aims to prevent the healthy flow of time, to dam all currents of change and thereby turn society into a lethally noxious swamp. As Adam Ferguson emphasized in the eighteenth century, mankind's "emblem is a passing stream, not a stagnating pool."[2] Many centuries before, the Hippocratic corpus already advised humans to avoid swamps as miasmic pits of disease, just as Socrates, in his conversation with Theaetetus, suggested that motion, not rest, is good for the body and soul, that "windless air and the calm sea" are sources of placid "stillness" (*hēsuchiai*) that "causes decay and destruction" (*Theat.* 153c).[3] Returning to the eighteenth century, we recall that Kant did indeed spot the path to perpetual peace, on a sign hanging outside a Dutch inn, depicting a graveyard. Until the time when we find our final repose, it is human nature to stand up and contribute to the unfolding of history. The swamp cannot support such audacious weight.

Although the battles may at times be unpleasant, a war on complacency would appear to be necessary. Yet how legitimate is this offensive? Is there any collateral damage that should be taken into account? Furthermore, would any attack not always already be a lost cause? For obvious reasons, complacency can never be vanquished entirely, for such a victory would pave new ground for complacency to seep in. By definition, one can never grow complacent in one's fight against complacency. One can never be exceedingly pleased with one's triumph over being exceedingly pleased.

This line of inquiry may be sharpened by characterizing complacency as a classical comportment. Is it desirable or even possible to militate against the allure of classicism, with its promise of universal validity, its belief in eternal truths? If excessive or delusional satisfaction is problematic, what about its opposite? Should exaggerated discomfort and unease, dissatisfaction and displacement be fully embraced without any hope of resolution? Even the most insistent philologists, by their very labor, authenticate the exceptional value of the classical texts they scrutinize. A complete disavowal of that on which one depends would clearly be disingenuous. In waging a war against complacency—against evenness and smoothness—the hypercritical may ultimately show themselves to be hypocritical to the extreme. Moreover, scholars who assume the capacity to plumb the depths of concealed meanings, hermeneuts of suspicion who claim to delve beneath the surface of discourse and uncover latent significance, often display smug arrogance. In the end, can complacency be so easily identified as a target of critique? Can one ever be sure that one's strategies against the nothing-more and the nothing-new of sterile classicism do not in themselves contribute to a larger problem?

The Golden Age

We may all be restless creatures by nature, yet it is precisely some manner of rest and tranquility that often defines the ultimate goal of our ambitions. The aspiration for freedom from labor and stress can be interpreted in a number of ways; for example, as a latent death drive bound for nirvana or as nostalgia for early childhood days of complete gratification—either conclusion would put insatiable workaholics squarely on the side of their complacent counterparts. The unstoppable drive of Citizen Kane begins and ends with Rosebud. In the current technologized age of astounding velocity, many people long for deceleration, for a more just economy of sustenance as opposed to a ruthless economy of maximization or optimization. Despite an ingrained work ethic, despite the praise reserved for indefatigable industry, many people are envious of lifestyles that appear to be at perfect peace, blaming themselves for living to work rather than working to live.

Popular novels and films are replete with burned-out protagonists who travel to exotic locations and keenly observe how other cultures allow for ways of life that appear to be less harried, more easygoing, more content with humble pleasures. Those who are overworked gaze yearningly at laid-back lifestyles and rhythms. More often than not, however, the charge of distorting the facts applies to the little regard, generally speaking, for the poverty and concomitant anxieties that might mar this picture of noble savagery. As Manfred Koch observes, "Those who are leading the simple life usually show no particular appreciation for it. The real fishermen and shepherds of this world look at their lives and do not find the happiness of simplicity as much as the necessity of deprivation. They want to participate in the prosperity of the industrial countries and do not worry about whether they would thereby lose their peace or, indeed, sell their souls. We tourists are the ones who are suffering from our crushing work ethic; we are the ones who project onto others our longing for a less stressful, less complicated life."[1]

Modernist accusations of complacency may be, indeed, only psychic projections foisted on others to circumvent that which is sensed and feared within—a pleasure in comfort and ease. Perhaps our restlessness, our implacable persistence to remain dissatisfied and strive ceaselessly for something more, something better, is possible only from a stable basis of satisfactory conditions.

Since the late eighteenth century, modern life has more or less benefited from significant reforms and freedoms. At least in the West, populations are no longer in thrall to arbitrary power. States endeavor to be governed by the rule of law. Rigid class distinctions have sufficiently worn away to allow greater social mobility. Prejudicial behavior and discrimination have become broadly unacceptable. Advances in medicine have considerably reduced infant mortality, stemming the tide of epidemics and infectious disease, and providing paths for increased longevity. Although imperfections and abuses still persist, democracy at least holds out the promise of leveling social distinctions and privileges. From a strictly technological perspective, human history has never witnessed such high degrees of comfort and convenience. Criticism and objections aside, we have created a feel-good, palliative world that is on the whole relatively painless, a world where one has come to expect widespread sensitivity, tolerance, and inoffensive behavior, endless amenities, facilitation, and instant gratification. Complacency would appear to have no place in contemporary culture, and yet the expectation of convenience and luxury has perhaps never been more prevalent. "'We have discovered happiness'—say the last humans and blink."[2] It is not difficult to recognize ourselves in Friedrich Nietzsche's famous characterization of "the last man," in his description of humanity at the end of a certain history, when all that needed to be accomplished has been accomplished. As Volker Demuth elaborates:

> The last man is not the one who carries on the ethnic, religious, or political struggles of the past. The last man is rather the antihero, a mediocre type in a society of the middle, arranged in a nicely equipped social peace that feels like the cushioned domestic landscape in one's home. He is surrounded by cultural and medial bustling which, between entertainment and shocking scandal, between distraction and arousal, binds all one's psycho-political energies together like chemical substances. The last man lets himself be pleased with the way his life looks, as if it took place in the best of all possible worlds.[3]

In the age of the last man, complacency is no longer a moral fault but rather a well-established norm perpetuating a life reduced to utilitarian and hedonistic aims.

Although Nietzsche characterized the last man with an eye to the mass production, colonialism, and international trade of the late nineteenth century, it is arguably our present era of technological innovation that has brought this species to near perfection. Digitization removes almost every kind of material resistance, allowing user-subjects to surf along the internet's *plateiai* at will. High-speed connectivity readily overcomes the limitations of physical distance and personal memory. It would appear that everything is available—accessible and consumable—at any time from any location. We seem to be living in a veritable paradise where difficult, torturous labor is no longer necessary, where abundant results are obtainable by means of a few effortless clicks.

After two and a half millennia, we may well be tempted into believing that we have attained one of the greatest of classical dreams, Hesiod's mythic golden age:

ὥστε θεοὶ δ᾽ ἔζωον ἀκηδέα θυμὸν ἔχοντες,
νόσφιν ἄτερ τε πόνου καὶ ὀιζύος· οὐδέ τι δειλόν
γῆρας ἐπῆν, αἰεὶ δὲ πόδας καὶ χεῖρας ὁμοῖοι
τέρποντ᾽ ἐν θαλίῃσι κακῶν ἔκτοσθεν ἁπάντων·
θνῇσκον δ᾽ ὥσθ᾽ ὕπνῳ δεδμημένοι· ἐσθλὰ δὲ πάντα
τοῖσιν ἔην· καρπὸν δ᾽ ἔφερε ζείδωρος ἄρουρα
αὐτομάτη πολλόν τε καὶ ἄφθονον· οἳ δ᾽ ἐθελημοὶ
ἥσυχοι ἔργ᾽ ἐνέμοντο σὺν ἐσθλοῖσιν πολέεσσιν.
ἀφνειοὶ μήλοισι, φίλοι μακάρεσσι θεοῖσιν.

(WORKS AND DAYS, 112–20)

Just like gods they lived with carefree spirit,
far removed from toil and hardship; wretched old age
did not assail them, but, always the same in their feet and hands,
they delighted in festivities lacking in all evils;
and they died as if overpowered by sleep; all good things
they had: the grain-giving field bore crops
of its own accord [automatē], plenty and ungrudging; and they
    willingly
peacefully shared the fruits of their labors together with many
    good things.
Rich in sheep, dear to the blessed gods.

The conditions listed in Hesiod's catalog offer an image of a world that is free from the faults and problems that beleaguer present reality. And this collective wish appears to be upon us or at least within reach: the convenience and ease, the promise of health and prosperity, the extraordinary profits and possessions acquired without toil—literally by means of a source that runs on its own, an ideal of automation (*automatē*) that reinforces the appeal of our machines—the benefits of free sharing, the lack of want, and the stability of perpetual peace: in sum, a life that pleases because it is so self-evidently pleasing.

Modernity may like to see itself as implacable, and yet it seems to have always been in thrall to the flatness that renders the world more calculable. The rise of European humanism is coincident with advances in perspective and cartography, two revolutionary technologies that reduce volume and depth to comprehensible surfaces. Planimetric grids order the globe to mark proprietary rights and inspire further conquests. The plenitude of the entire world, across epochs and cultures, its history and its aspirations, comes to be displayed visually and textually on the flatness of the page. At the height of the Enlightenment, in introducing the *Encyclopédie*, Jean Le Rond d'Alembert expresses the dream of universal tabulation upon a single plane. Today's screen technologies and networks continue a trend that has long been in place, breeding general gratification with ever thinner, more efficient devices that deceive most of us into believing that nothing is taking place within or behind them.[4]

Speed ranks supreme and depends on unobstructed channels and clear transmission, which hark back to conventional modes of travel. As B. W. Highman explains in *Flatness*, "Rapid motion depends on movement across a smooth/flat surface. If the surface is irregular or rough, motion is impeded by friction, and the bumpiness of the passage will discomfort the traveler, just as will happen if the passage bounces erratically from side to side by deviating from a forward-moving straight-line route."[5] With flatness, we acquire not only greater velocity but also a higher degree of predictability, which is what one should expect from well-laid plans. Still, one might sense some concern, the troubling sense that predictability and planiformity also entail monotony and boredom.[6] A fundamentally implacable, anticlassical nature might resist surrendering to such global convenience.

Institutions

By nature, institutions tend to promote complacency, even if they provide sure ground for productive enterprises. As mechanisms for organizing social activity, institutional structures exhibit the kind of stable persistence that could encourage uncritical behavior, groupthink, and perfunctory responses. Although they rely on the vigilance and adroitness of their employees, large corporations, like the modern administrative state, function by means of basic frameworks, procedures, and policies that maintain what has worked in the past, at times despite clear pressures and demands from without. The temptation to proceed on autopilot is great, if only because it relieves individuals of personal responsibility. Substantial change at these basic levels is highly complex and difficult, making organizations less capable of addressing unaccustomed problems or adapting to unfamiliar situations. Bureaucracy tends to strangle innovative approaches; ingrained conduct squashes ingenuity; and real improvement—if room for improvement is even acknowledged—turns out to be nearly impossible.

Academic institutions are, of course, no exception. Even the most liberal-minded teachers still betray conservatism when it comes to institutional policies and principles. Impassioned advocates for thinking differently, for challenging preconceptions and overturning received opinion, might all the same defy any sort of radical change, such as eliminating established departments or redesigning the university's divisions.

Again, there is no threat of complacency when one is satisfied with conventions that actually yield satisfactory outcomes. Drastic revisions should be executed only in response to unsatisfactory circumstances, and not simply for the sake of change. That said, arguments adduced to uphold long-standing structures ring empty when they offer nothing more than mere tautologies—for example, when they insist on the worth of what is already in place merely because it has long been in place. Thus, calls for safeguarding tenure are altogether legitimate when they seek to defend academic freedom from ideological censorship or to ensure competitive faculty recruitment, yet complacency can always creep in as soon as professors take advantage of permanent job security to cover their incompetence, idleness, or complete indifference to their students or the university's educational mission.

Explicitly designed to avoid the debilitating snare of stagnation and negligence, modern educational systems have long fostered ongoing enrichment and steady maturation. Ever since the rise of humanism and scientific empiricism, restless if not aggressive curiosity has been fully exonerated, promulgated as a virtue to be nourished rather than as a sinful perversion to be condemned. The aspiration to make ever new discoveries has definitively outpaced complacent satisfaction with what is already possessed. As the title of Nicholas Cusanus's 1488 treatise *De venatione sapientiae* already suggests, thinking and learning are akin to hunting, driven by an intellectual hunger that can never be quelled. For Francis Bacon, writing more than a century later, the imperative for every student is clear: "one does not rest, but rather discovers that he should seek further."[1] The Enlightenment set perpetual striving and progress as core features of human existence. And today, we continue to endorse these precepts by rewarding ambition, productivity, and unflagging industriousness. The premise throughout is to forge ahead, to face whatever challenges may occur, to welcome every defeat as a fresh opportunity. We are encouraged to be strong and adaptable, resilient and versatile. At all costs, one should never give up, one should never look back, one should never plummet into a state of useless indolence.

Nonetheless, our educational institutions may at times be seen as abandoning these core ideals. Cordoned off from the profane world of industry, commerce, and day-to-day affairs, colleges have long been suspected of being places of useless inactivity. The ancient Greek conception of "school" already denotes "leisure" or "idleness" (*scholē*). This designation, however, can be understood in at least two ways. On the one hand, in being divorced from quotidian concerns, the scholar is said to occupy a position endowed with critical power. Here, the leisure denoted by *scholē* provides a crucial opportunity, whereby one can take time off to study what is truly important as opposed to what is merely urgent. Scholarly *otium* frees us from the distraction of *busyness* which, in Latin as well as in Greek, is conceived explicitly as the negation of leisure: *negotium, ascholia*.

On the other hand, commonly from an outsider's perspective, those who are ensconced in their ivied or ivory towers are open to the charge of resting snugly in the comfort of their thoughts. Particularly in the United States, elites and pundits are often vilified for being uninformed, for being so pleased with their explanatory models that they fail to understand what is actually happening in society at large. There is extraordinary glee whenever an academic prediction proves false or whenever professors are exposed as self-serving hypocrites.

Perhaps today's efforts to transform university programs into practically useful enterprises is but an embarrassed defense against the charge of indolence, an apotropaic gesture designed to ward off public attacks or prove them otherwise. Especially in an age of neoliberalism, by showing a commitment to prepare students for the needs of the workplace, the university aims to show that it is capable of *negotiating* with society in a decisively direct fashion. It may well be a vestigial fear of damnation that drives academics to blur the line between contemplative study and active labor, to calibrate research with social issues and national initiatives, with policy making and the profit-driven ventures of the business sector—all as a way of checking a deeply embedded proclivity to sin.

Scaling back humanities programs, or at least revising their scope, frequently emerges as an almost unavoidable consequence of these ambitions. More and more, the promotion of science and technology, engineering and mathematics, is viewed as an urgent corrective, designed to combat academic complacency and thereby ensure the advancement of the new and the more. Scientific positivism should be prioritized over critical negativity. This trend is already discernible within the humanities, and not only in the adoption of digital tools and methods. Creative writing and art making are gaining an upper hand over literary history and interpretation. Symptomatic reading—with its assumption that the text conceals more than it says, with its call for the excavation of hidden or repressed content—is now yielding to "surface reading," which gathers information that is accessible in plain view.[2] Thus, the virtues of praxis might dissuade one from the vices of theory. Yet, can the mantra of positivism—"it is what it is"—ever be distinguished from the very complacency it seeks to attack?

The Humanities

Shallow, blotching, blundering, infectious "information"
JOHN RUSKIN, *SESAME AND LILIES*

The discipline of classics always risks complacency whenever it presumes classical prestige. As soon as it rests content with an immutable canon of works, once it restricts itself to an aesthetic ideology of set rules and exclusionary criteria, the academic study of the ancient world rouses grave suspicions and invites broad contempt, both within and beyond the university. In retailing a system of standards purported to be timeless, universal, and unimpeachable, classicism appears to disregard any contingency or aspect of relativity, for fear that it would compromise the absolutism of its sacred ideals. Thus, scholars of the past who appealed to a classicizing program stood to be accused of being not only elitist, irrelevant, impractical, racist, or fetishistic, but also remarkably self-delusional, mired in a sterile vision of their own construction that distracts them from present realities and diverse perspectives, trapped in a planned economy of sense.

Historically, the antidote for this debility has been some conception of science. Over the last two centuries, scientific approaches have been adduced to check classicizing presumptions that hinder progress. Celebrated for being value-free, a scientific outlook is thought to represent open-minded objectivity, unrestrained by subjective or ideological bias. Whereas the complacent classicist seeks only that which will confirm prior judgments, the implacable scientist remains receptive to revising or even discarding established explanations in pursuit of truth. With scientific neutrality, the canon loses its supervisory function, presuppositions are shattered, and reformulations are deemed urgently necessary. Thus, by the mid-nineteenth century, the classical curriculum that once defined higher education in antebellum America and Victorian England eventually succumbed to trends of increasing professionalization ascribed to Germanic philology. A reassertion of the value of textual criticism, historicist scrutiny, and exacting methodology unsettled abstract pontifications on beauty and virtue. Tireless labor *supplanted* timeless aspirations. Calls for rigorous training superseded concerns for molding moral character and refining sensibilities, for populating polite society or breeding colonial administrators.

Today, with the help of science, the discipline of classics in the modern research university has, indeed, liberated itself from the straitjacket of reactionary complacency. Since the 1980s, the field has expanded significantly, becoming ever more inclusive, pluralistic, and interdisciplinary. The study of texts and materials that fall beyond the traditional core of fifth-century Athens and late republican, early imperial Rome, the attention to everyday life, women, and marginalized classes in antiquity, the adoption of new theoretical paradigms, the acknowledgment of the value of long reception histories—these reconfigurations all mark important innovations that overturn conventional modes of thinking and interpretation.

Yet, has the scientific reliance on experimentation, observation, and measurement been sufficient for rousing classics from its former parochialism and intellectual torpor, for stimulating enough dissatisfaction to ensure the discipline's continued productivity and pertinence? Natural and social scientists are, after all, hardly immune to complacent tendencies, just as their procedures cannot be entirely exonerated of value judgments and subjective bias. Particularly when focused on operational or applied procedures, the sciences often betray the same desire for smoothness and comprehensibility, not in terms of eternal ideals of beauty and virtue, but rather in terms of technological progress, which promises greater certainty, well-being, and convenience. If classicism once protected a ruling class from the menacing aura of difference, scientific operationalism now preserves its adherents from the threat of other, equally threatening anxieties.

Although fully grounded in a humanist tradition, classical conservatives appear to be guilty of instituting an intellectual complacency that glosses over historical and cultural variance; and scientific positivism seems to behave classically by striving to establish truths that would be unaffected by diachronic shifts in language or problems of untranslatability. Chemists hardly need to consider whether the properties of nitrogen have changed over time, just as pupils of mathematics can trust that the square root of 16 is always 4, whether one expresses it in English, Russian, or Swahili. In analogous ways, classicists once regarded symmetry, balanced proportion, and aesthetic unity as irrefutable truths. Moreover, the technological assumption that the new is always better would appear to be as misguided as the conservative insistence that the old is always superior. In the end, coasting along the flattened plane of presentism may not be any different from gliding across the evened field of anti-quarianism.

In particular, the scientific insistence on *relevance* betrays a classicizing wish to *relieve* (*relevare*) problems, to lighten the load and thus ease the path toward the attainment of proven, objective knowledge. Relevance is a desideratum that regards every problem as a problem to be solved. Of course, science would achieve no progress whatsoever if it allowed prior results to remain unquestioned. Yet the drive behind the mathematizable sciences is to recalculate and revise, with the aim of discovering less assailable determinations, to smooth out troublesome hindrances, and to arrive at conclusions that will withstand the test of time. In face of such ambition, history becomes but a series of ultimately dispensable attempts, moving constantly and teleologically toward firmer certitude. Classicism was generally fueled by the same desire to transcend historical qualifications and contingencies.

Philology, too, can become trapped in the dead end of academic complacency whenever it claims for itself an unassailable capacity for securing authorial intention and establishing a text's definitive sense. Philological complacency enlists knowledge as an end in itself rather than as a basis for ongoing investigation, interrogation, and interpretation. As James Porter explains, traditional philology entails an "agency that helps to sustain the mythical shape of the present, in part by alienating myth as an object of dispassionate study," as opposed to the critical philology that Porter discerns in Friedrich Nietzsche's praxis, one that proves itself to be "a self-reflexive, self-critical, and often paradoxical undertaking."[1] This latter "philology of the future" never idles complacently inasmuch as it orients itself toward the provisionality of open-ended time, rather than continuing routinely with present concepts and presuppositions.[2]

Critical philology turns to both classics and science for its content and methodology, respectively; yet it does so without the scientific and classicizing demand for atemporal, transhistorical validity. Instead, it maintains a commitment to historical and cultural difference, turning the history of a problem into a problem in its own right. Here, any leveling out would be suspected of acquiescing to solutions that abstract themes from their concrete emergence and development, their reorientation and transformation.

As a reading practice, critical philology approaches a text as a field that invites passage. The *page* is likened to a country "province" (*pagus*) to be crossed. At times the terrain appears to be perfectly flat and smooth, allowing for easy transit; yet at other times the road to sense is rocky and more difficult. Whereas some readers wish to move briskly across a text, leaping over annoying frustrations, eager to reach the planned destination, the critical philologist relishes in the interruptions. Whereas other readers may travel in a more leisurely manner, pausing with pleasure to admire the idiosyncrasies of the verbal path, the philologist hesitates even longer, concerned more with how the meaning is being conveyed. As always, philology is called on to consider each word—every syllable, every letter—as a problem that demands serious attention: as a *problēma* or a large stone that has been thrown on the track. The temptation is to break these obdurate masses open, to reveal what might rest within; or perhaps to dig deeper, to move downward, realizing that many of these verbal stones reach far below the surface of the text, hidden from direct view and thus requiring additional exertion and special tools.

*

With reportedly waning student interest in the humanities, one has heard an oft-repeated diagnosis—that humanists themselves are responsible for the downturn. The merciless interrogation of every posited value, the deconstruction of every text, the radical relativism that borders on complete nihilism—all have supposedly contributed to the lukewarm reception of the humanities among today's student body. In his popular study *Education's End: Why Our Colleges and Universities Have Given Up on the Meaning of Life* (2009), Anthony Kronman places the

fault on humanists who have abandoned what they are particularly equipped to do: to introduce young minds to the major
themes that define human existence and thereby allow students to enter the "great conversation" with "poets, philosophers, novelists, historians, and artists" reaching back to the
ancient Greeks.[3] Yet even if humanist scholars today could forgo
the philological commitment to the constructivism, multicul-
turalism, and historical relativism implicit in their methods,
it is still not certain that more great books courses would be a
sufficient strategy to redeem their fields from the lower ranks
among the faculties.[4]

A classical curriculum in the traditional sense would not be
able to speak broadly enough to a diverse student body in a tech-
nocratic world. A more likely path for redemption might be the
so-called digital humanities insofar as these lines of inquiry and
verification emerge from new technological resources and platforms. The many evangelists of new media point to the collection
and analysis of big data, which offer insights that would otherwise remain impossible for any single scholar unaided by digital
tools. Refined algorithmic procedures and innovative modeling,
together with expanded networks, social media, and globally
interconnected classrooms, have indeed had a revolutionary
effect on the production and transmission of higher learning. In
terms of comprehensiveness and accessibility, digital archives
far exceed the limits of personal libraries, just as search engines
clearly surpass individual mental capacities. Global connectivity flattens the world, conquering the many inconveniences,
obstacles, and injustices that come with geographical distance.

Critics of digitization, however, frequently attack the homog-
enizing effects of new media, where everything is produced,
transmitted, and disseminated on the screen, where material
resistance is practically eliminated, where temporality col-
lapses into the presumed immediacy of the present. Scientific

appeals to universal, mathematizable laws degenerate into unreflective presentism. Digital platforms are seen as electronic *plateiai*, designed for around-the-clock commerce, consumption, and self-flattery. Flat surfaces invite readers to skim briskly and superficially, rather than penetrate deeply. Human consciousness itself appears to have been pushed to the surface, fascinated by the planar sheen of a mirror stage, without recourse to the symbolic resources that relate the visible to the invisible.

Such fascination may promulgate subjectivity without interiority. In Peter Sloterdijk's terms, the "technological turn" is responsible for turning "reader subjectivity" into "user subjectivity": "The user does not stop collecting . . . but what they collect are not experiences, in the sense of personally integrated, narratively and conceptually ordered complexes of knowledge; they are addresses where knowledge aggregates formed to varying extents can be found, should one wish to access them for whatever reason."[5] The negative force of otherness and radical difference seems to be erased in favor of the kind of pleasing diversity that can be accommodated into an efficient system of conformity. The result is classicizing, and in a decidedly antiphilological mode: "Natural languages are a nuisance for those who propagate the view that we all have to move far more: they are offended by these sluggish symbolic systems, as they do not readily submit to the demand for compression and acceleration."[6] Learning languages takes up too much precious time; it is hardly worth the trouble, especially now that machine translation is becoming ever more refined and accurate. Digitization brings welcome *relief*. Yet, when learning and research become fully reliant on technological operatives and automatic retrieval, they seem to depart ever further from lived experience. Difficulty is no longer appreciated as a productive complication but rather as an annoying hindrance.

These estimations edge into social critiques against a society where connections appear to trump relationships, where friends are counted without being physically encountered. Serious engagement has been replaced by "likes." The thumbs-up icon expresses a state of being pleased without serious engagement. Individuals travel great distances and partake in spectacular adventures, while sitting quietly before their screens in nearly perfect isolation.[7] The subject's transcendence has never been more secure. Inflated self-images are promoted and distributed which loom much larger than a wolf's shadow on the plain. According to this critique, the posthuman has filled the vacuum left by the exit of the humanities: genetics replaces the conscious will, artificial intelligence supplants human cognition, databases are consulted instead of subjective reason and memory, tweeting reduces speech to the level of mere platitude. The implication is that we have arrived at a new complacency by resting content in an unarticulated present or unquestioned past, ambling upon a flattened world.

Anthropologically, bumps in the field of thinking can be regarded as the raised thresholds that feature in every rite of passage to represent a nonterminal death—the death of the old self, which is prerequisite for rebirth. A leveled place removes the raised hurdles that are necessary for transformation; and without the possibility for transformation, information remains mere information: positive facts that are accumulated and counted, gleaned from an impersonal web, without the negative opacity or mysterious core that resides beneath and within every face-to-face encounter. We may become overly content to collect information in an additive fashion along a horizontal plane that lies before us—a plane that does not existentially implicate us—passing laterally from one screen to the next, while growing ever more incapable of the selective work that organizes and prioritizes facts on a vertical axis. Metonymy outpaces metaphor.

Still, flatness can have beneficial results, which digital technology no doubt affords. Without volume or depth, flatness dismantles asymmetrical power relations and hierarchies. Everything is laid out in the open, creating a new transparency that would expose any and all abusers. Two-dimensionality does not allow for the interior, secret reserve on which power always depends. Thus, Gilles Deleuze and Félix Guattari deploy a conception of the "plateau" where multiplicities laterally connect with other multiplicities, producing a "rhizome" of superficialities that eliminates any orthogonal anchoring in a single, authoritative source.[8] Similarly, Manuel DeLanda has called for a "flat ontology" out of respect for the unique singularity of individual entities, liberated from categorizations that invariably impose hierarchical strata.[9] On a more quotidian level, we know that games should be performed on leveled fields or flat boards, so as to create similar conditions of equality.[10] A level area is required for a fair and exciting match; one cannot play tennis on a court riddled with mounds. All forms of meritocracy depend on an even playing field, where everyone has an equal chance to succeed, to win.

Bourgeois mentality has always insisted on this kind of flatness—the refusal to grant undue privilege on the basis of birth or familial relationships, cultural or racial identity. Yet taken too far, one can become complacent in believing that life is truly a fair game, simply a matter of competition and keeping score, of pulling oneself up by the bootstraps. One may complacently believe that asymmetrical power, injustice, and contingencies of birth play no role when in point of fact they do. We can pretend, for as long as we wish, that our involvement with digital platforms is untroubled by concealed marketing tactics or invasive surveillance, that there are no ravenous lions lying in wait, ever ready to pounce.

If we are, in fact, living in an era of classical, technologi-

cal complacency—in a fool's paradise of convenient accessibility and functionality—then critical philology can furnish an
urgent corrective, not on the basis of authority but rather on
the promise expressed by its love for the word, its *philia* for the
logos, an intimate friendship that should balk at any attempt to
gain full possession and full control over the object of its longing. As a practice that has historically disrupted the easy glide
across the two-dimensional page, philology may adduce just the
right amount of difficulty and inconvenience that instigates
critique. Philological attentiveness has always energized classics by inculcating a refusal to be pleased with the face value of
discursive-textual histories, by triggering a dissatisfaction that
demands probing beneath the classical façade, not to destroy its
values but rather to uphold them as altogether provisional, by
investigating the latent meanings, metaphors, and images of
other epochs, cultures, and lifeworlds. Philology is both profane
and profound, exhibiting a capacity to dive below the gleaming
surface and plumb the depths, to pursue the temporal traces
that render languages dynamic and unwieldy, to prevent words
from resting pleasantly in place. At the very least, philology provides a potent reminder that the entrance fee to eternal paradise has always required a *sacrifice*, a *making-sacred* that consists of fatal determinations and terminal stillness.

Notes

EPIGRAPH

1 Guillevic, "Plane (I)," *Geometries*, trans. Richard Sieburth (New York: Ugly Duckling Presse, 2010).

THE WOLF ON THE PLAIN

1 Fable 260, in Perry, *Aesopica*, 422. Unless otherwise noted, all translations are mine.

2 See Perry, *Babrius and Phaedrus*, xlvii–lv.

3 Rutherford, *Babrius*, v.

4 For an excellent discussion, see Arruzza, "The Lion and the Wolf."

5 See, for example, Watkins, *American Heritage Dictionary of Indo-European Roots*, 70, s.v. *plāk-¹*. Watkins bases his conjectures on those listed in Pokorny, *Indogermanisches etymologisches Wörterbuch*, 832–33.

6 For a useful account on etymologizing and paronomasia in antiquity, see Maltby, "Limits of Etymologising."

7 On the hazards of *authadeia*, see Plato, *Rep.* 8.548e and 9.590a; Aristotle, *Eud. Eth.* 1233b35ff and *Mag. Mor.* 1192b31ff; Theophrastus, *Char.* 15; Plutarch, *Pol. Prec.* 808d; and Aelius Aristides, *Orat.* 23.

SINS IN THE ACADEMY

1 Blackburn quoted in Reisz, "Seven Deadly Sins of the Academy."

2 Blackburn quoted in Reisz.

3 Blackburn quoted in Reisz.

4 Stray, "Culture and Discipline," 77.

COLONIAL PLANNING

1 Trevelyan, *Competition Wallah*, 246–47.
2 Cf. Hagerman, *Britain's Imperial Muse*, 2–3.
3 Abbott, *Annotated Flatland*, 155.
4 See Ian Stewart's introduction to Abbott, *Annotated Flatland*, xviii–xx.
5 Abbott, *Annotated Flatland*, 24.

PROPOSITIONAL SURFACES

1 Shakespeare, *Complete Works*, 1351. See Blackburn, *Ruling Passions*, 9.
2 Blackburn, 4–8.
3 McDowell outlines his sensibility theory in "Non-Cognitivism and Rule-Following" (1981), reprinted in McDowell, *Mind, Value, and Reality*, 198–218. For a comprehensive assessment of Blackburn's issues and their limitations, see Ross and Turner, "Sensibility Theory and Conservative Complacency."
4 McDowell, *Mind, Value, and Reality*, 206–7, citing Cavell, *Must We Mean What We Say?* 52.
5 Blackburn, *Ruling Passions*, 101.
6 Blackburn, 101–2.
7 Blackburn, 103.
8 Blackburn, "Securing the Nots," 83–84.

CLASSICAL PLATFORMS

1 See Porter, "What Is 'Classical' about Classical Antiquity?"
2 Corneille, *Discours de la tragédie.*
3 On the tension between classics as a reinforcement of conservatism and its revolutionary potential, see Goldhill, *Victorian Culture and Classical Antiquity*, 1–9.
4 In this regard, noncomplacent classicism represents the kind of humanism that Charles Martindale accords to vital reception, one that can allow us "to escape our routinized habits." Martindale, "Reception—A New Humanism?" 179.
5 As Hartmut Böhme comments, "Culture is the art (*ars, technē*) by which societies secure their survival and their development in an overpowering nature." Böhme, "Vom Cultus zur Kultur(wissenschaft)," 52.

6 Arnold, *Culture and Anarchy*, 50.
7 Boileau-Despréaux, *Œuvres*, 188.
8 Boileau-Despréaux, 77.
9 Boileau-Despréaux, 77.
10 Boileau-Despréaux, 77.

PHILOLOGY AS *ANCILLA FACULTATUM*

1 Kermode, *Classic*, 68.
2 Eliot, *What Is a Classic?* 31–32.
3 Bettini, *Classical Indiscretions*, 74.
4 See my elaboration on this figure in Hamilton, *Philology of the Flesh*, 73–75.
5 For further discussion on the contrast between philosophy and philology, see Kraye, "Philologists and Philosophers"; Turner, *Philology*, 33–39; and Hamilton, *Philology of the Flesh*, 121–57.
6 On this important tension, see Güthenke, "'Enthusiasm Dwells Only in Specialization.'"
7 John Grote, "Old Studies and New," in *Cambridge Essays, 1856* (London: Parker, 1856), 114, cited in Stray, "Culture and Discipline," 82.
8 R. M. Milnes, Lord Houghton, "The Dilettanti Society," *Edinburgh Review* 105 (1857): 493–517, cited in Stray, "Culture and Discipline," 82.

PHILOLOGICAL INVESTIGATIONS

1 In the modern European translations, including the King James Bible, it is Psalm 77.
2 See Crowe, "Complacency and Concern in the Thought of St. Thomas," 1:20–23.
3 Aquinas, *Summa Theologiae*, part 1.2, question 26, article 1c, quoted in Crowe, 1:22.
4 Aquinas, *Summa Theologiae*, pt. 1.2, quest. 25, art. 2c, quoted in Crowe, 1:26.
5 For a comprehensive discussion, including significant reflections on later philosophical developments of the theme, see Crowe.
6 *Traité de l'amour de Dieu*, 5.3, in de Sales, *Traité de l'amour de Dieu*, 266.
7 Hobbes, *Leviathan*, 76.
8 *Guardian*, no. 162 (September 16, 1713), in Addison, *Works of Joseph Addison*, 3:840.

9 Addison, *Works*, 3:840–41.

10 Osland, "Complaisance and Complacence," 493.

11 Immanuel Kant, *Reflexionen zur Anthropologie*, §655, in Kant, *Gesammelte Schriften*, 15:41.

12 Kant, *Gesammelte Schriften*, 15:270.

13 Kant, *Anthropologie in pragmatischer Hinsicht*, §69, in Kant, *Gesammelte Schriften*, 7:244.

PLEASINGLY FLAT

1 The most recent work in historical linguistics distinguishes four, unrelated roots: *$pleth_2$*- (spread out) in Greek *platus*; *$pleh_2$*- or *$pelh_2$*- (flat) in Latin *planus*; *$plek$*- (to plait), which may be related to Greek *plax, plakos*; and *$plak$*- (to be pleasing, agree) in Latin *placere*. See the pertinent entries in de Vaan, *Etymological Dictionary of Latin*. Still, speculation on an all-encompassing root *$plā$-k*- is to be found in Pokorny, *Indogermanisches etymologisches Wörterbuch*, 1:831–32, s.v. *$plā$-k*-; and in Watkins, *American Heritage Dictionary of Indo-European Roots*, 70, s.v. *$plāk$*-.

2 For a useful overview and discussion, see Emile Benveniste, "La phrase nominale," in Benveniste, *Problèmes de linguistique générale*, 1:151–67.

3 On a possible etymological link between *pulcher* and *placere*, see Hasse, "Pulcher. Gnavus."

4 Joyce, *Portrait of the Artist as a Young Man*, 186.

5 In this regard, the present study pursues the methods of metaphorology as articulated in the work of Hans Blumenberg. On this point, see Blumenberg, *Paradigms for a Metaphorology*.

PLATEA

1 For a comprehensive and scrupulous account, with ample bibliography, see Casey, *Fate of Place*. My brief sketch here summarizes Casey's general account.

2 Dey, "From 'Street' to 'Piazza,'" 919.

3 Cf. Zeller, "Vicus, platea, platiodanni."

4 See Harsh, "Angiportum, Platea, and Vicus."

THE WAR ON COMPLACENCY

1 Cf. Kawall, "On Complacency," 350.
2 Ferguson, *History of Civil Society*, 11.
3 Cf. Konersmann, *Unruhe der Welt*, 182.

THE GOLDEN AGE

1 Koch, *Faulheit*, 12.
2 Nietzsche, *Also sprach Zarathustra*, 284.
3 Demuth, *Der nächste Mensch*, 11.
4 On all these points, see Connor, "Flat Life."
5 Highman, *Flatness*, 87.
6 See Highman, 102.

INSTITUTIONS

1 Bacon, "Praefatio," in *Novum organum*, quoted in Konersmann, *Unruhe der Welt*, 31–35.
2 See Best and Marcus, "Surface Reading."

THE HUMANITIES

1 Porter, *Nietzsche and the Philology of the Future*, 224.
2 This antinormative version of the philological impulse is fully explored in Hamacher, *Minima Philologica*.
3 Kronman, *Education's End*, 85.
4 On the historically fraught relationship between the discipline of classics and great books curricula in American academia, see Adler, *Classics, the Culture Wars, and Beyond*, 43–76.
5 Sloterdijk, *In the World Interior of Capital*, 219.
6 Sloterdijk, 260.
7 On this and similar lines of critique, see Han, *Im Schwarm*.
8 See Deleuze and Guattari, *A Thousand Plateaus*, 22.
9 DeLanda, *Intensive Science and Virtual Philosophy*, 47.
10 See Connor, "Flat Life."

Works Cited

Abbott, Edwin A. *The Annotated Flatland: A Romance of Many Dimensions.* With introduction and notes by Ian Stewart. New York: Basic Books, 2002.

Addison, Joseph. *The Works of Joseph Addison.* 5 vols. Edited by George W. Greene. New York: Putnam, 1853.

Adler, Eric. *Classics, the Culture Wars, and Beyond.* Ann Arbor: University of Michigan Press, 2016.

Arnold, Matthew. *Culture and Anarchy.* Edited by Stefan Collini. Cambridge: Cambridge University Press, 1993. First published 1869.

Arruzza, Cinzia. "The Lion and the Wolf: The Tyrant's Spirit in Plato's *Republic,*" *Ancient Philosophy* 38, no. 1 (Spring 2018): 47–67.

Bacon, Francis. *Novum organum.* Edited by Thomas Fowler. Oxford: Clarendon Press, 1878. First published 1620.

Best, Stephen, and Sharon Marcus. "Surface Reading: An Introduction." *Representations* 108 (2009): 1–21.

Benveniste, Emile. *Problèmes de linguistique générale.* 2 vols. Paris: Gallimard, 1966.

Bettini, Maurizio. *Classical Indiscretions: A Millennial Enquiry into the Status of the Classics.* Translated by John McManamon. London: Duckworth, 2001.

Blackburn, Simon. *Ruling Passions: A Theory of Practical Reasoning.* Oxford: Clarendon Press, 1998.

———. "Securing the Nots: Moral Epistemology for the Quasi-Realist." In *Moral Knowledge? New Readings in Moral Epistemology*, edited by Walter Sinnott-Armstrong and Mark Timmons, 82–100. Oxford: Oxford University Press, 1996.

Blumenberg, Hans. *Paradigms for a Metaphorology.* Translated by Robert Savage. Ithaca, NY: Cornell University Press, 2016.

Böhme, Hartmut. "Vom Cultus zur Kultur(wissenschaft): Zur historischen Semantik des Kulturbegriffs." In *Kulturwissenschaft–*

Literaturwissenschaft: Positionen. Themen. Perspektiven, edited by Renate Glaser and Matthias Luserke, 48–68. Opladen, Ger.: Westdeutscher Verlag, 1996.

Boileau-Despréaux, Nicolas. *Œuvres*. Edited by M. Amar. Paris: Didot, 1860.

Casey, Edward S. *The Fate of Place: A Philosophical History*. Berkeley: University of California Press, 1997.

Cavell, Stanley. *Must We Mean What We Say?* New York: Scribner's, 1969.

Connor, Steven. "Flat Life." Steven Conner (website). Accessed July 7, 2021. http://stevenconnor.com/flat.html.

Corneille, Pierre. *Discours de la tragédie* [1660]. In *Œuvres*, vol. 1, edited by Charles Louandre. Paris: Charpentier, 1853.

Crowe, Frederick. "Complacency and Concern in the Thought of St. Thomas," *Theological Studies* 20, nos. 1–3 (1959): 1–39, 198–230, 343–95.

DeLanda, Manuel. *Intensive Science and Virtual Philosophy*. New York: Bloomsbury, 2002.

Deleuze, Gilles, and Félix Guattari. *A Thousand Plateaus: Capitalism and Schizophrenia*. Translated by Brian Massumi. Minneapolis: University of Minnesota Press, 1987.

Demuth, Volker. *Der nächste Mensch*. Berlin: Matthes & Seitz, 2018.

de Sales, Francis. *Traité de l'amour de Dieu*. Edited by Bonvalet des Brosses. Paris: Saintmichel, 1813.

de Vaan, Michael. *Etymological Dictionary of Latin and Other Italic Languages*. Leiden, Neth.: Brill, 2008.

Dey, Hendrick. "From 'Street' to 'Piazza': Urban Politics, Public Ceremony, and the Redefinition of *platea* in Communal Italy and Beyond." *Speculum* 91, no. 4 (October 2016): 919–44.

Eliot, T. S. *What Is a Classic?* London: Faber & Faber, 1945.

Ferguson, Adam. *An Essay on the History of Civil Society*. 5th ed. London: Cadell, 1782. First published 1767. Page references are to the 1782 edition.

Goldhill, Simon. *Victorian Culture and Classical Antiquity*. Princeton, NJ: Princeton University Press, 2011.

Güthenke, Constanze. "'Enthusiasm Dwells Only in Specialization': Classical Philology and Disciplinarity in Nineteenth-Century Germany." In *World Philology*, edited by Sheldon Pollock, Benjamin A. Elman, and Ku-ming Kevin Chang, 264–84. Cambridge, MA: Harvard University Press, 2015.

Hagerman, Christopher. *Britain's Imperial Muse: The Classics, Imperialism, and the Indian Empire, 1784–1914*. New York: Palgrave Macmillan, 2013.

Hamacher, Werner. *Minima Philologica*. Translated by Catharine Diehl and Jason Groves. New York: Fordham University Press, 2015.

Hamilton, John T. *Philology of the Flesh*. Chicago: University of Chicago Press, 2018.

Han, Byung-Chul. *Im Schwarm: Ansichten des Digitalen*. Berlin: Matthes & Seitz, 2013.

Harsh, Philip W. "Angiportum, Platea, and Vicus." *Classical Philology* 32, no. 1 (January 1937): 44–58.

Hasse, Ernst. "Pulcher. Gnavus." *Glotta* 3, no. 3 (1911): 276–77.

Highman, B. W. *Flatness*. London: Reaktion, 2017.

Hobbes, Thomas. *Leviathan, or the Matter, Form, & Power of a Commonwealth Ecclesiastical and Civil*. In *The Clarendon Edition of the Works of Thomas Hobbes*, vols. 3–5. Oxford: Clarendon Press, 2012. First published 1651. Page references are to the 2012 edition.

Joyce, James. *Portrait of the Artist as a Young Man*. Edited by Chester G. Anderson. New York: Viking, 1968.

Kant, Immanuel. *Gesammelte Schriften* (Akademie-Ausgabe) [Complete works (Akademie Edition)]. 23 vols. Berlin: de Gruyter, 1922.

Kawall, Jason. "On Complacency." *American Philosophical Quarterly* 43, no. 4 (October 2006): 343–55.

Kermode, Frank. *The Classic: Literary Images of Permanence and Change*. Rev. ed. Cambridge, MA: Harvard University Press, 1983.

Koch, Manfred. *Faulheit: Eine schwierige Disziplin*. Springe, Ger.: zu Klampen, 2012.

Konersmann, Ralf. *Unruhe der Welt*. Frankfurt am Main: Fischer, 2015.

Kraye, Jill. "Philologists and Philosophers." In *The Cambridge Companion to Renaissance Humanism*, edited by Jill Kraye, 142–60. Cambridge: Cambridge University Press, 2006.

Kronman, Anthony. *Education's End: Why Our Colleges and Universities Have Given Up on the Meaning of Life*. New Haven, CT: Yale University Press, 2009.

Maltby, Robert. "The Limits of Etymologising." *Aevum Antiquum* 6 (1993): 257–75.

Martindale, Charles. "Reception—A New Humanism? Receptivity, Pedagogy, the Transhistorical." *Classical Receptions Journal* 5, no. 2 (2013): 169–83.

McDowell, John. *Mind, Value, and Reality*. Cambridge, MA: Harvard University Press, 1998.

Nietzsche, Friedrich. *Also sprach Zarathustra*. In *Werke*, vol. 2, edited by Karl Schlechta. Munich: Hanser, 1966.

Osland, Diane. "Complaisance and Complacence, and the Perils of Pleasing in *Clarissa*," *Studies in English Literature* 40, no. 3 (Summer 2000): 491–509.

Perry, Ben Edwin, ed. *Aesopica*. 2nd edition. New York: Arno Press, 1980.

———. *Babrius and Phaedrus*. Cambridge, MA: Harvard University Press, 1965.

Pokorny, Julius. *Indogermanisches etymologisches Wörterbuch*. Bern, Switz.: Francke, 1959.

———. *Nietzsche and the Philology of the Future*. Stanford, CA: Stanford University Press, 2000.

———. "What Is 'Classical' about Classical Antiquity? Eight Propositions." *Arion* 13, no. 1 (2005): 27–61.

Reisz, Matthew. "The Seven Deadly Sins of the Academy." *Times Higher Education*, September 17, 2009. https://www.timeshighereducation.co.uk/features/the-seven-deadly-sins-of-the-academy/408135. article.

Ross, Peter, and Dale Turner. "Sensibility Theory and Conservative Complacency," *Pacific Philosophical Quarterly* 86, no. 4 (2005): 544–55.

Rutherford, W. Gunion. *Babrius*. London: Macmillan, 1883.

Shakespeare, William. *The Complete Works*. New Pelican Text. Edited by Stephen Orgel and A. R. Braunmuller. New York: Penguin, 2002.

Sloterdijk, Peter. *In the World Interior of Capital: Towards a Philosophical Theory of Globalization*. Translated by Wieland Hoban. Cambridge: Polity, 2013.

Stray, Christopher. "Culture and Discipline: Classics and Society in Victorian England." *International Journal of the Classical Tradition* 3, no. 1 (1996): 77–85.

Turner, James. *Philology: The Forgotten Origins of the Modern Humanities*. Princeton, NJ: Princeton University Press, 2014.

Trevelyan, George Otto. *The Competition Wallah*. London: Macmillan, 1864.

Watkins, Calvert, ed. *The American Heritage Dictionary of Indo-European Roots*. 3rd ed. New York: Houghton Mifflin Harcourt, 2011.

Zeller, Joseph. "Vicus, platea, platiodanni." *Archiv für lateinische Lexicographie* 14 (1905): 301–16.

Index